P:D:A:T:E

Managing
river environments

Geraldene Wharton

CAMBRIDGE
UNIVERSITY PRESS

PUBLISHED BY THE PRESS SYNDICATE OF THE UNIVERSITY OF CAMBRIDGE
The Pitt Building, Trumpington Street, Cambridge, United Kingdom

CAMBRIDGE UNIVERSITY PRESS
The Edinburgh Building, Cambridge CB2 2RU, UK   http://www.cup.cam.ac.uk
40 West 20th Street, New York, NY 10011-4211, USA   http://www.cup.org
10 Stamford Road, Oakleigh, Melbourne 3166, Australia
Ruiz de Alarcón 13, 28014 Madrid, Spain

First published 2000

Printed in Great Britain at the University Press, Cambridge

Typeface *Times*   System *Pagemaker 6.5®*

A catalogue record for this book is available from the British Library

ISBN 0 521 45854 4 paperback

The author

Dr Geraldene Wharton is a lecturer in physical geography and environmental science in the Departmen
of Geography at Queen Mary and Westfield College, University of London, where she teaches courses
hydrology, river processes and river management, and researches into river restoration and flood
estimation. The author's first degree (Sheffield University) and PhD (Southampton University) are in
geography. She has been Secretary to the Geography Section of the British Association for the
Advancement of Science (1994–98), and has recently been elected on to the Council of the Royal
Geographical Society (with Institute of British Geographers) as Honorary Secretary of the Education
Division.

Update

Update is a unique project in educational publishing. It is aimed at A-level students and first-year
undergraduates in geography. The objective of the series, which ranges across both physical and huma
geography, is to combine the study of major issues in the geography syllabus with accounts of especia
significant case studies. Each *Update* tries to incorporate a large amount of empirical material presente
in easy-to-read tables, maps and diagrams.

Update is produced from the Department of Geography at Queen Mary and Westfield College, Unive
of London. The editorial board comprises a team from across the fields of geography and education:
Bruce Atkinson, Roger Lee, Geraldene Wharton (editor) and Edward Oliver (cartographer) from QM
and David Lambert, Sheila King and David Job from the Institute of Education (Department of
Geography).

We hope that you find the series as exciting to use as we find it to produce. The editor would be deli
to receive any suggestions for further *Updates* or comments on how we could make the series even
useful.

*Cover: People try to make their way through the flood water in a submerged district of Tangail, 72
kilometres (45 miles) north of Dhaka, 11 September 1998. The devastating flood is thought to have
claimed more than 850 lives and affected some 35 million people. (AP Photo/Pavel Rahman)*

Contents

iv

Acknowledgements

I am indebted to Professor K. J. Gregory and Dr A. D. Knighton for introducing me to the fascination and the challenge of fluvial research. I have also drawn tremendous inspiration from Dr Andrew Brookes' writings on river management. At the time of beginning to prepare this *Update*, Brookes' text *Channelized Rivers – Perspectives for Environmental Management* was the only comprehensive study of channelisation and I found it impossible to improve upon the logical structure of considering traditional techniques, impacts and finally new approaches which Brookes (1988) employed. As a consequence, Chapters 3, 4 and 5 follow this sequence.

Thanks are also recorded to Andrew Brookes and David Sear for supplying photographs (Andrew Brookes: Plates 3.1, 3.8, 3.10. David Sear: Plate 3.7). All other photos are provided by the author.

I am particularly grateful for all the information and advice given to me in preparing this volume, although I bear sole responsibility for any errors in the text. Special thanks are recorded to Edward Oliver, cartographer in the Department of Geography, for his work on the figures, tables and overall design of this *Update*.

The author and publishers would like to thank the following for permission to use copyright material in this book:

Academic Press Ltd for our figure 4.6 originally from Brookes (1987a), and for our figure 5.6 originally from Swales (1982b); American Society of Agricultural Engineers for our figure 4.4 originally from Campbell *et al.* (1972); American Society of Civil Engineers for our figure 4.2 originally from Parker and Andres (1976), for our figure 5.11 originally from Keller and Brookes (1984), and for our figure 5.14 originally from Keller and Brookes (1984); Andrew Brookes for information in our tables 4.2 and 4.4 originally from Brookes (1983); Blackwell Publishers for our figure 6.2 originally from Newson (1977 p. 167), our figure 6.8 originally from Goudie (1993 p. 355), our figure 6.9 originally from Goudie (1993 p. 356), and our figure 6.11 originally from Goudie (1993 p. 358); Edward Arnold for our figure 2.1 adapted from original in Knighton (1998 p. 2), our figure 2.5d originally from Knighton (1984 p. 149), our figure 2.6 originally from Knighton (1998 p. 158), and our figure 2.7 originally from Knighton (1984 p. 91); Environment Agency for our figure 3.2 originally from British Hydrological Society (1994 pp. 3–4, copyright © Environment Agency), for our figure 1.3 originally from Environment Agency (1996b p. 64, copyright © Environment Agency), and for information in our Appendix 1 originally from Environment Agency (1996a, copyright © Environment Agency); Haslam, S. M. and Wolseley, P. A. for our figure 2.3 originally from Haslam and Wolseley (1981 p. 25 and p. 47); IAHS Press for our figure 6.14 originally from Palutikov (1987); John Wiley and Sons, Inc. for our figure 2.10 originally from Kochel (1988 p. 184); John Wiley and Sons Ltd for our figure 1.1 originally in Winkley (1982), our figure 4.1 originally in Brookes (1988 p. 23), our figure 4.3 originally in Brookes (1987c), our figure 4.5 originally in Brookes (1988 p. 112), our figure 5.5 originally in Brookes (1988 p. 213), our figure 5.13 originally in Petersen *et al.* (1992 p. 300), our table 3.1 originally in Brookes (1988 p. 32), our table 3.2 originally in Brookes (1988 p. 34), our table 4.3 originally in Brookes (1988 p. 126) and our table 5.1 originally in Brookes (1988 p. 206); Ken Gregory and Des Walling for our figure 2.2 originally from Gregory and Walling (1973 p. 10); Longman for our table 2.1 originally from Morisawa (1985 p. 12), our table 2.2 originally from Morisawa (1985 p. 13), and our figure 2.5c originally from Morisawa (1985 p. 90); National Academy Press for our figure 6.7 originally in Stern *et al.* (1992 p. 29), our table 6.3 originally in Stern *et al.* (1992 p. 50), and our table 6.4 originally in Revelle and Waggoner (1983); *Nature* for our figure 6.10 originally from Wigley *et al.* (1980); Oxford University Press for our figure 3.4 originally from Purseglove (1989 p. 213), for our figure 5.2 originally from Purseglove (1989 p. 170), our figure 5.3 originally from Purseglove (1989 p. 182), our figure 5.7a originally from Purseglove (1989 p. 173) and our figure 5.10 originally from Purseglove (1989 p. 180); Rita Gardner for our figure 6.3 originally from Gardner (1994 p. 3); River Restoration Centre for our information in Appendix 2; Routledge (Unwin Hyman) for our figure 2.5a originally from Briggs and Smithson (1985 p. 343) and for our figure 2.9, adapted from original in Briggs and Smithson (1985 p. 220); Routledge, for our figure 6.1 originally from Newson (1997 p. xxix), and our figure 6.2 originally from Newson (1997 p. 167); Royal Geographical Society for our figure 6.6 and information in our case study originally from Kimmage and Adams (1992); *Scotland on Sunday* for our figure 6.5 and case study originally from *Scotland on Sunday* (16 June 1996 p. 19); Scottish Environment Protection Agency (SEPA) for our figure 1.4 originally from SEPA (1996) and for information in our Appendix 1; Springer-Verlag for our figure 5.16 originally from Brookes (1987b); Swedish Society for Anthropology and Geography (Blackwell Publishers) for our figure 2.4 originally in Ashworth and Ferguson (1986); the *Guardian* for our figure 3.3 originally from the *Guardian* (11 January 1994 p. 18); The Royal Society for the Protection of Birds for our figure 5.4 originally from RSPB, NRA & RSNC (1994 pp. 288–9), our figure 5.7b originally from RSPB, NRA & RSNC (1994 p. 347) and our case study including figure 5.12 originally from RSPB, NRA & RSNC (1994 p. 361); and The University of Arizona Press for our figure 6.13 originally from Budyko and Izrael (1991).

Every effort has been made to reach copyright holders. The publisher would be pleased to hear from anyone whose rights they have unwittingly infringed.

1 Introduction

- *Why have river environments been developed and modified?*

- *How widespread is river channelisation?*

- *Why is the study of river channelisation so important?*

- *Who is responsible for river management, and what laws control it?*

1.1 About this book

River environments are arguably one of the most exploited of all natural environments. The reasons are simple. Rivers provide a water supply to domestic and industrial users, they are employed for shipping and waste disposal, they are fished, mined for gravel and harnessed for their renewable energy, and they are an important recreational resource. The adjacent fertile floodplains are highly prized for agriculture; they also provide accessible routes for land-based transport and flat building land. And, as the world population continues to increase, pressures for floodplain development escalate.

To facilitate this development and sustain the exploitation of river environments, river flows have been regulated through the construction of dams, and river *channels* have been engineered (see box for definition of channelisation). However, floods cause more deaths and result in more destruction than any other natural disaster, and damages from flooding continue to increase. Is this evidence that structural approaches to flood management are not working? Furthermore, in recent decades there has been growing concern over the consequences of traditional river engineering, and a realisation that rivers cannot be fully 'tamed'. This has led to calls for a much greater understanding of river processes as a basis for sympathetic river designs and sustainable management. River channelisation is thus an important environmental, social and economic issue. This acknowledged need for a more effective approach to river and catchment management is the central theme of this *Update*.

Geographers, primarily geomorphologists, and environmental scientists are now playing a key role in river channel management. The value of geomorphology is in understanding the factors contributing to the stability and instability of natural river channels (Chapter 2) and in anticipating the consequences of particular engineering projects (Chapter 4). Geomorphology has also proved successful in developing alternative designs and strategies that work *with* nature rather than *against* it. These new approaches to river management are discussed in Chapters 5 and 6. Whilst river regulation has been important for flood control in many countries (see Petts, 1984 for a comprehensive review), I have chosen to focus on management which has been achieved through direct modifications to river channels (channnelisation) because this is the major type of river engineering throughout the UK and indeed most of lowland western Europe.

Channelisation is the term used to describe the alteration of river channels by engineering for the purposes of flood control, drainage improvement, reduction of bank erosion, maintenance of navigation or relocation for highway construction (Brookes, 1988, p. 5). Channelisation may also be associated with programmes for draining fields or forested areas, and in Scandinavia watercourses have been cleared and straightened in order to float logs out from forests.

1.2 A brief history of river channelisation

The origins of river channelisation can be traced to 6000 BC when Mesopotamia and Egypt managed water supplies and practised flood control to sustain settled agriculture. By 2500 BC, the Egyptians had developed a very powerful civilisation in the Indus basin based on river engineering works. In China, reaches of the Huang He (Yellow River) were embanked as early as 600 BC, and in Britain the Romans constructed embankments to protect low-lying marsh areas in the Fens and Somerset Levels from flooding.

Despite these early beginnings and the unique importance of rivers to a nation's development, the history and geographical extent of river channelisation is poorly documented for most countries. The USA, Great Britain and Denmark are three exceptions.

1.2.1 Channelisation in the USA

Channelisation started to become widespread in the USA in the nineteenth century, and in the past 150 years at least 320,000 km of rivers have been modified in some way to drain land for agriculture, control floods and to provide for river shipping. The early river works were highly fragmented, being carried out by states, counties, towns, local districts, individuals and private companies. At the present time, there are two principal agencies engaged in channelisation: the Corps of Engineers, empowered under the Flood Control Acts of 1936 and 1944, and the Soil Conservation Service, which carries out small projects under the Watershed Protection and Flood Prevention Act of 1954 (Brookes, 1988, p. 9).

Channelisation has not taken place evenly along America's rivers. Instead it has been prevalent in a few states: 65 per cent of all channel alteration work is concentrated in Illinois, Indiana, North Dakota, Ohio and Kansas, with 51 per cent of levee work in California, Illinois and Florida. This concentration reflects the counties suffering historically from the most severe land drainage and flood problems (Brookes, 1988, p. 10).

In the early nineteenth century much of the land in the American Mid-West, especially in Iowa and east-central Illinois, suffered from poor drainage which caused swampy conditions and crop failures, and encouraged mosquitoes. Extensive channel improvements and the construction of drainage ditches converted swamp into rich cropland. In the Vermillion River watershed in east-central Illinois, a staggering 105 legal drainage districts were created between 1880 and 1974 to implement the operations (Brookes, 1988, p. 9).

Flood control has been equally important in the development of the USA. Streams were straightened in California as early as 1871 by farmers and ranchers employing Chinese labourers and using horse-drawn equipment to excavate the channels. The flood hazard, however, remains a major national problem with about 7 per cent of the USA (541, 310 km²) subject to inundation by

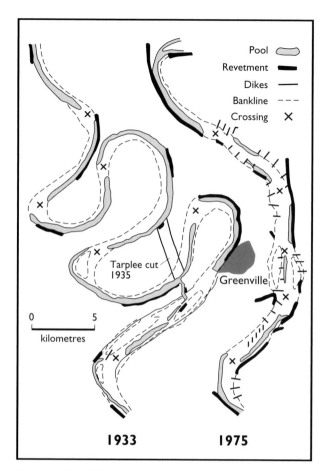

Figure 1.1 The Greenville reach on the Mississippi river Source: Winkley, 1982.

the 100-year flood. Using the 1970 census and land data, Goddard (1976) estimated there to be about 22,000 flood-prone communities and 42,730 km² of urban floodplain in the USA, covering a total of 6.4 million single family homes (Brookes, 1988, p. 11). Since 1953 there have been over 375 national disasters caused by flooding, the 1993 Mississippi floods being the most recent, and on average 100 people die each year from flooding (Costa, 1978).

1.2.2 Channelisation of the Mississippi River

The Mississippi is 3,219 km long, drains half of the USA and is one of the most heavily engineered rivers in the world. To the developers and engineers the river presented two major problems. It shifted its course constantly, by eroding its banks and forming and reforming huge sand bars, and it flooded onto the surrounding wetlands each spring. The river was dangerous and unpredictable for navigation, and flood control was necessary to develop the floodplain for farming and industry.

To clear a navigable route, the Mississippi had to be deepened to at least 2.75 m along its entire length. Dredging on that scale was not possible, so the Corps of Engineers installed some structures in

Table 1.1   **Channelisation history of the Mississippi River**

Pre-nineteenth century	Principal channel works involved the removal of sediment deposits and caving river banks.
1800s	Steamboats directly caused the clearance of thousands of hectares of streambank vegetation (leaving river banks unprotected).
1811 and 1812	Major earthquakes caused excessive bank collapse and increased the sediment in the river. Channel deposits caused problems for river navigation.
1819 onwards	Levees constructed which confined floodwaters but increased sediment movement downstream.
1879	Congress established the Mississippi River Commission.
1884	Large-scale bank protection programme initiated to restrict normal migration of the channel and prevent river cutoffs forming.
1895	Dredging for navigation began but caused further problems by releasing more sediment downstream.
late 1800s	River training structures introduced to promote local bed scouring and deposition.
1927	Major flood event.
1930s and 1940s	River shortened by 243 km using cutoffs as a flood control measure (to reduce flood levels, eliminate erosion and increase sediment transport). However, to maintain the alignment of the river following cutoffs, it was essential to dredge continuously for a period of more than 10 years, especially in the straightened reaches. Over 1,300 million m^3 of sediment were removed to maintain navigation.
1945 to 1970	Dikes and revetments were constructed to protect the channel banks from erosion.

Source: information from Brookes, 1988, pp. 18–20.

the channel called *dikes* (also known as groynes). The dikes led to channel narrowing and forced the river to dig a deeper channel along the opposite bank to the dikes. By constantly building and rebuilding the dikes in different places, as the river shifted, the engineers have maintained the navigation channel.

In an attempt to solve the flood problem, land was cleared along the whole length of the Mississippi, and levees – massive earth and clay banks – were constructed to contain the floods. In addition, more than 200 flood-control reservoirs were built to hold back floodwaters and prevent the levees collapsing under the pressure of exceptional floods.

To aid river navigation and flood control the Corps of Engineers also straightened and shortened the river by bypassing all the tortuous river meanders. At completion in 1942 the river was 241 km

shorter. The straightening substantially reduced the shipping route and also speeded up the flow of water downstream, thereby lowering flood levels in the engineered river reaches.

This was not the end of the river engineering, however. To stabilise the river and prevent it from trying to meander again, the Corps of Engineers developed a unique machine which could assemble and lay a mattress of concrete slabs along the river bed in a single automated system. In one day this machine could line 10 acres of river with concrete (Horizon, 1994). The Greenville reach (Figure 1.1) is one such straightened and shortened reach (from 82 to 32 km) now restrained by concrete revetments and dikes.

The engineering of the Mississippi has taken over 100 years to complete (Table 1.1), at a cost of over US$10 billion, and it takes over US$180 million a year just to maintain the control structures. However, without the levees, the cities, farms and factories on the floodplain would never have been built, and without the dikes the shipping industry would not exist.

1.2.3 Channelisation in Great Britain

River channel modifications have been carried out in Britain for at least 2,000 years, and the different types of channelisation over time reflect the changing uses of rivers and their environments. Small-scale river works have been undertaken since the earliest cultivation and first settlements. Streams were realigned to run along fields or to act as boundaries between individual farms, and riverside vegetation was cleared to create rough pasture or meadow. Where the floodplains of large watercourses were required for cultivation, the rivers were diverted or impounded over short lengths to irrigate water meadows or to provide power for small watermills. As towns and cities developed, small streams were confined to underground pipes. However, it has been the modification of rivers for navigation and the widespread drainage of floodplains and lowlands that have been the two main driving forces behind river engineering in Great Britain.

Navigation. Dredging was employed in the late fourteenth and fifteenth centuries to aid navigation because of the extensive silting of rivers thought to have been the result of deforestation. Mechanisation provided further impetus in the seventeenth century and many patents were taken out for dredgers. For example, on 16 July 1618 John Gilbert took out a patent for a water plough for taking up sand and gravel, and there is evidence that it made great holes in the bed of the River Thames.

During the period from 1600 to 1750 major improvements such as river widening and deepening became inevitable following the substantial growth of population in England and the increased demands for essential commodities. Cutoffs, to shorten river lengths, became a widely used method in the seventeenth century. The River Wey navigation, built in the 1600s, involved extensive cuts; of the total length of 24 km, 11 km consisted of artificial cuts. Such channel straightening necessitated bank protection, and stakes made from alder branches were widely used. After 1760, river transport switched to artificial canals and the alteration of rivers for navigation became less important.

Land drainage. Significant land drainage and flood control have been carried out in Britain during the past 550 years but two periods of drainage stand out. The need to increase agricultural production to feed a growing urban population triggered the first phase of activity in the 1840s. This was aided by the arrival of the steam pump which was much more efficient than wind or animal-drawn pumps. The Land Drainage Act (1861) is perhaps the most notable landmark in the history of land drainage in Britain. The Act permitted the maintenance and improvement of existing drainage works and the construction of new works.

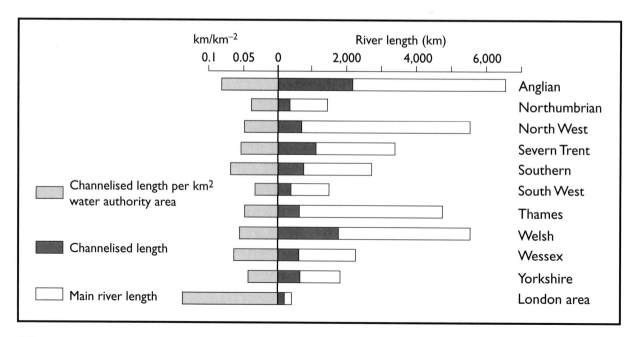

Figure 1.2   Channelised river lengths in England and Wales by water authority area
    Source: Brookes *et al.*, 1983.

During the Second World War Britain needed to become self-sufficient in food. This required a further phase of drainage of low-lying land, including river floodplains, to intensify farming in these areas. Farming typically changed from low-input grazing to intensive cereal production. In the immediate post-war period the River Boards Act 1948 created 32 River Boards and River Board Areas for the management and implementation of drainage schemes. Pressures for intensification of farming remained and further changes have continued to take place in the administration of land drainage. Land drainage in England and Wales is now controlled by the Environment Agency.

Current extent of channelisation. The extent of channel works has been established for England and Wales by Brookes (1983) for the period 1930–80. A total of 8,500 km of main rivers in England and Wales have undergone major river engineering that has a lasting impact on channel morphology, and a further 35,500 km of river channel are regularly maintained by dredging and weed cutting. Figure 1.2 highlights how regions with large residential and industrial areas or intensive agriculture have the highest proportions of channelised river.

1.2.4 Channelisation in Denmark

Channelisation has been most prolific in developed countries in both urban and rural areas, and its extent is directly related to the intensity of land use. Thus in many West European lowland countries (which are even more intensively farmed than Britain) such as Denmark, The Netherlands and northern Belgium, channelisation has been extensive.

The notion of modifying river channels for the purpose of agricultural drainage in Denmark was implicit in early parliamentary legislation, including the Watercourse Law of 1846. A century later, The Watercourse Act of 1949, with amendments in 1963, 1965, 1969 and 1973, gave drainage priority over any other river use, so that activities which would come into conflict with land drainage required the special permission of a Watercourse Tribunal (Brookes, 1988, p. 17).

The natural river-bed forms, such as pools and riffles, and aquatic vegetation on the bed and along the banks of a river were regarded as obstructions which impeded drainage. Under the Act, rules relating to the maintenance of public rivers were laid down in a series of 'Regulatives' which defined the river's course, its dimensions (width and depth) and the elevation above sea-level. These regulations also specified the times of the year when maintenance should be undertaken to control the water level. Importantly, the regulations do not cover the management of private rivers in Denmark, which are the responsibility of the riparian owners.

The amount of channelisation in Denmark has been investigated using information collated from maps, field surveys and engineering documents (Brookes, 1987c). It is estimated that 97.8 per cent of all streams had been straightened by 1987, which is equivalent to a density of modified water-courses of 0.9 km km^{-2}. This compares with a density of channelised river in England and Wales of 0.06 (Brookes *et al.*, 1983) and 0.003 for the USA (Leopold, 1977). Thus Denmark has a density of channelised river 15 times greater than England and Wales and 300 times greater than the USA.

1.3 River management legislation in Great Britain

In 1991 the then Prime Minister John Major announced the setting up of an Environment Agency, and began to consult on its purpose and organisation. Four years later the Environment Bill 1995 received Royal Assent and led to the establishment of two new Non-Departmental Public Bodies – the Environment Agency for England and Wales (EA) and the Scottish Environmental Protection Agency (SEPA) (see Appendix 1). Although there are many similarities between the SEPA and the EA, there are two important differences: the SEPA does not have a land drainage function, and ministers have not taken the opportunity to introduce more comprehensive control of water abstraction in Scotland (SEPA, 1996).

1.3.1 The Environment Agency

The EA is sponsored by the Department of the Environment with policy links to the Welsh Office and the Ministry of Agriculture, Fisheries and Food. The EA combines the regulation and management of land, air and water resources in England and Wales by taking over the functions of its predecessors the National Rivers Authority (NRA), Her Majesty's Inspectorate of Pollution (HMIP), Waste Regulation Authorities (WRAs) and some parts of the Department of the Environment.

Principal aims and objectives. The Environment Agency defines its principle aim as follows:

> 'in discharging its functions the Agency is required so to protect or enhance the environment, taken as a whole, as to make the contribution that Ministers consider appropriate towards achieving sustainable development' (Environment Agency Customer Charter, May 1996).

The Agency's overall aim of protecting and enhancing the whole environment contributes to the world-wide environmental goal of sustainable development, which has been defined by the Chief Executive of the EA, Ed Gallagher, as 'development that meets the needs of the present without compromising the ability of future generations to meet their own needs' (Environment Agency, 1996a).

It is proposed that the EA works towards sustainable development through seven objectives, set by Ministers and reported in the Agency's Customer Charter (1996a):

- An integrated approach to environmental protections and enhancement, considering the impact of all activities and natural resources.
- Delivery of environmental goals without imposing disproportionate costs on industry or society as a whole.
- Clear and effective procedures for serving its customers, including the development of single points of contact with the Agency.
- High professional standards, using the best information and analytical methods.
- Organisation of its own activities to reflect good environmental and management practices, and provision of value for money for those who pay its charges, and for taxpayers as a whole.
- Provision of clear and readily available advice and information on its work.
- Development of a close and responsive relationship with the public, including Local Authorities, other representatives of local communities and regulated organisations.

The Environment Agency is also committed to a number of important principles, including the Precautionary Principle, and Best Environmental Practice (see box).

The work of the EA is divided into seven main functions – flood defence, water resources, pollution control (including water regulation),

---

> ***Precautionary Principle*** **– to be prepared to take precautionary action where there are significant risks of damage to the environment from the Agency's own activities, to limit the use of potentially dangerous materials, or the spread of potentially dangerous pollutants, even where scientific knowledge is not conclusive, if the balance of likely costs and benefits justifies it.**
>
> ***Best Environmental Practice*** **– to develop, demonstrate, promote and monitor the use of integrated environmentally sustainable best practice, techniques and management throughout its own activities, by considering the direct and indirect effects and the use of resources, and the impacts of releases on all environmental media. The EA is committed to adopting a holistic approach to flood prevention management.**

Source: *The Environmental Policy for the Agency's Own Activities.* Information supplied by the Environment Agency of England and Wales with the Customer Charter (EA, 1996a).

fisheries, navigation, recreation, and conservation. These categories correspond almost entirely with the former NRA functions. All aspects of the Agency's work (see Appendix 1 for details) are potentially important in river management.

Organisation and structure. There are eight EA Regions (Figure 1.3) with a Head Office (see Appendix 1 for address), eight Regional Offices and Area Offices within each Region. Regions are split into three or four Areas making a total of 26. The Agency has a Board of up to 15 members appointed by the Department of the Environment, the Ministry of Agriculture, Fisheries and Food, and the Welsh Office; the Board includes the Agency's Chairman and Chief Executive. Eight directors provide overall management of the Agency's work and are based at the Head Office in Bristol with supporting offices in London. Each Region has a Regional General Manager with three statutory Regional Committees, including local authority and business representatives, and covering environmental protection, flood defence and fisheries matters. Regional committee meetings are open to the public and the media. Each Area also has a Manager to ensure that local community requirements and concerns are considered.

Table 1.2   **SEPA's inherited duties and powers and new provisions that relate to river management**

Inherited duties and powers

- consenting to discharges to the water environment
- conserving water resources as far as possible
- providing flood warning systems
- granting abstraction licences for irrigation where a control order is in force
- issuing authorisations to prevent, minimise or render harmless the release of substances into the environment from prescribed processes
- monitoring of pollution
- enforced action against persons breaching licence conditions or illegally polluting the environment

New provisions

- a function to assess, as far as appropriate, risk of flooding in any area
- a duty to advise planning authorities on flood risk
- status as a statutory consultee on new land drainage works
- a duty to promote the conservation and enhancement of the natural beauty and amenity of controlled waters
- powers to carry out assessments of the general state of the environment

Source: Background information on SEPA supplied by SEPA's Head Office in Stirling, April 1996.

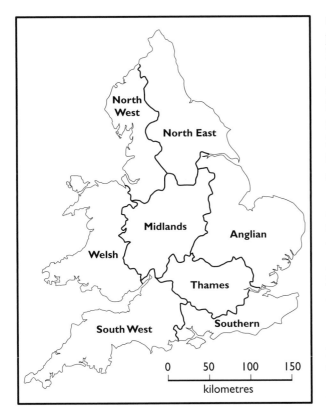

Figure 1.3   Environment Agency Regions
Source: Environment Agency, 1996a.

1.3.2   The Scottish Environment Protection Agency

The Scottish Environment Protection Agency (SEPA) was formed from the amalgamation of seven River Purification Boards and the river purification functions undertaken by the three Islands Councils, Her Majesty's Industrial Pollution Inspectorate, and the waste regulation and local air pollution functions of the District and Islands Councils. It has also taken over many of the duties of the Hazardous Waste Inspectorate. SEPA comprises the Chairman, Deputy Chairman, Chief Executive and nine other Members, and is accountable to the Secretary of State for Scotland.

Principal aims and objectives. SEPA's principal task is to protect land, air and water and to work with others to help Scotland achieve economic growth that is both strong and sustainable, but it must also have regard to guidance issued by the Secretary of State for Scotland.

SEPA has inherited a large number of duties and powers from the well-established predecessor organisations but the Environment Act 1995 also gave SEPA several new provisions (Table 1.2). Most importantly, the new legislation requires SEPA to provide guidance on flood risk to planning authorities, when consulted, and it is hoped that this will develop into a more active role in flood risk assessment.

Organisation and structure. SEPA's Head Office is in Stirling and provides support and policy direction for the three Regions which are

Table 1.3   **Environmental legislation and European Community Directives relevant to river management in England and Wales**

The key environmental legislation includes:

- Environment Act, 1995
- Wildlife and Countryside Act, 1981
- Water Resources Act, 1991, Sections 2(2), 16 and 17
- Land Drainage Act, 1991, Sections 12 and 13
- Land Drainage Improvement Works (Assessment of Environmental Effects) Regulations SI 1988 No 1217
- Town and Country Planning (Assessment of Environmental Effects) Regulations SI 1988 No 1199
- Town and Country Planning (Listed Buildings and Conservation Areas) Act, 1990
- Ancient Monuments and Archaeological Areas Act, 1979

The European Community Directives include:

- Council Directive 79/409/EEC on the conservation of wild birds
- Council Directive 85/337/EEC on the assessment of the environmental effects of certain public and private projects on the environment
- Council Directive 92/43/EEC on the conservation of natural habitats and of wild fauna and flora

Source: *Environmental Procedures for Inland Flood Defence Works* (1992, p. 11) published by the Ministry of Agriculture, Fisheries and Food, English Nature, National Rivers Authority, Royal Society for the Protection of Birds, in consultation with the Welsh Office, the Countryside Council for Wales and other environmental organisations and operating authorities.

responsible for all operations of the new body (Figure 1.4). The Regions operate through a network of three regional and 17 local offices throughout Scotland.

The East Region covers the areas of the Tweed, Forth and Tay River Purification Boards and includes the new unitary authorities of Scottish Borders, East Lothian, West Lothian, Midlothian, City of Edinburgh, Falkirk, Fife, Clackmannanshire, Stirling, Perth & Kinross, Angus, Dundee City and a small part of Aberdeenshire.

The North Region covers the areas for the North East and Highland River Purification Boards and the Western Isles, Orkney and Shetland, and includes the new unitary authorities of Aberdeenshire, Aberdeen City, Moray, Highland, Western Isles, Orkney and Shetland.

The West Region covers the areas of the Solway and Clyde River Purification Boards and includes the new unitary authorities of Dumfries & Galloway, North, South and East Ayrshire, North and South Lanarkshire, Inverclyde, East Renfrewshire, Glasgow City, East Dunbartonshire, West Dunbartonshire, Renfrewshire, Argyll & Bute, and small parts of Scottish Borders, Stirling and Highland.

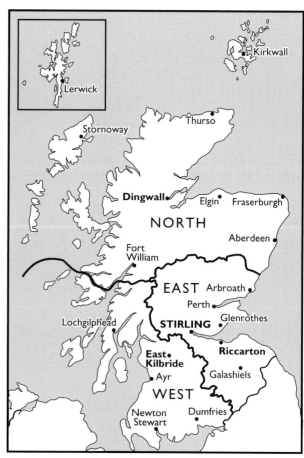

Figure 1.4   Scottish Environment Protection Agency Regions and network of regional and local offices
Source: Scottish Environment Protection Agency, 1996.

Table 1.4 **Bodies for consultation for new river works or improvements to existing flood defence / land drainage works**

- Nature Conservancy Council for England (NCCE) or the Countryside Council for Wales (CCW)
- Broads Authority
- National Parks Authorities
- Countryside Commission (CC) in England or the CCW (in Wales)
- English Heritage (in England) or Cadw (in Wales)

Other bodies' interests might also be affected and they should likewise be consulted where applicable either directly or through the bodies listed above, for example:

- local authorities on conservation, archaeological, landscape and access issues
- Royal Society for Nature Conservation, Wildlife Trust Partnership
- county sites and Monuments Records Offices
- National Trust
- Regional Welsh Archaeological Trusts
- Council for the Protection of Rural England
- Council for the Protection of Rural Wales
- Royal Society for the Protection of Birds
- Council for British Archaeology
- Water Services Association Working Party on Industrial Archaeology
- other local amenity and conservation organisations.

Source: *Conservation Guidelines for Drainage Authorities* (1991, pp. 12–13) prepared by the Ministry of Agriculture, Fisheries and Food in association with the Department of Transport and the Welsh Office.

1.3.3 Further legislation

In addition to the recent Environment Act 1995 there is a large amount of legislation which governs river management activities; the main Acts are listed in Table 1.3. The Water Resources Act 1991 and Land Drainage Act 1991 are particularly important. Section 16 of the Water Resources Act 1991 and Section 12 of the Land Drainage Act 1991 impose a duty to:

i   further the conservation and enhancement of natural beauty, consistent with any enactments relating to their functions;

ii   further the conservation of wildlife and geological and physiographical features of special interest, consistent with any enactments relating to their functions;

iii   have regard to the desirability of:

(a) protecting and conserving buildings, sites and objects of archaeological, architectural or historical interest; and

(b) preserving public rights of access to areas of mountains, moor, heath, down, cliff or foreshore and other places of natural beauty;

iv   take into account the effects of any proposals on the preservation of rights of access and on the beauty or amenity of an area, or on wildlife, features, buildings, sites or objects.

Section 2(2) of the Water Resources Act 1991 also imposes a duty to promote:

i   the conservation and enhancement of the natural beauty and amenity of inland and coastal waters and of land associated with such waters; and

ii   the conservation of flora and fauna which are dependent on an aquatic environment.

To minimise the environmental impact of their own proposals the EA and SEPA should also consult widely before carrying out any work (see Table 1.4) and take particular care where operations may affect directly or indirectly any protected areas (Figure 1.5) or protected sites as follows:

- Biosphere Reserves (an international network of protected areas launched by UNESCO);
- Ramsar Sites (wetlands of international importance);
- Special Protection Areas (SPAs) designated or proposed for designation under the European

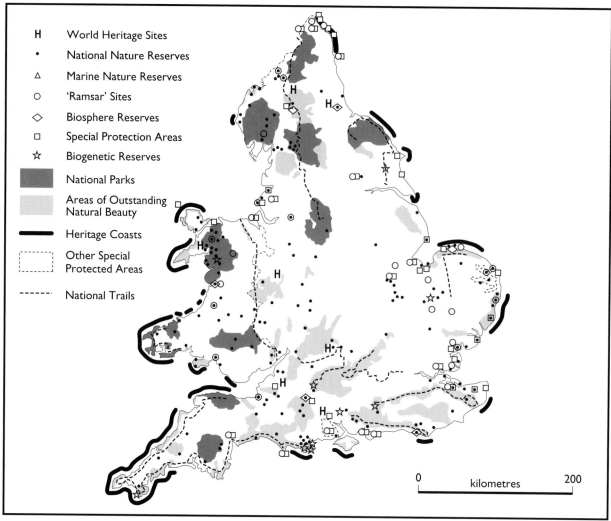

Figure 1.5   Protected areas in England and Wales
Source: Environment Agency, 1996b, p. 64.

Community's Council Directive 79/409/EEC on the conservation of wild birds;

- species protected under the Wildlife and Countryside Act 1981 (as amended);
- Sites of Special Scientific Interest (SSSIs);
- Environmentally Sensitive Areas (ESAs);
- national and local Nature Reserves;
- ancient monuments;
- listed buildings;
- National Parks;
- Areas of Outstanding Natural Beauty;
- Heritage Coasts;
- Public Rights of Way; and
- any other sites of environmental or archaeological interest such as those identified by Local Authorities and those owned or managed by the National Trust or voluntary conservation agencies.

The European Union (EU) also has a significant effect on British environmental (including river) legislation through a series of Directives (Table 1.3), which cover many subjects including water quality, waste disposal, chemical emissions, wildlife protection, countryside management, sewage disposal, nitrates, phosphates and wildlife habitats (Brown and Howell, 1992, p. 410). For example, the EU's Council Directive 85/337/EEC sets out the arrangements for the environmental impact assessment of public and private river projects and the preparation of an Environmental Statement. This is a publicly available document setting out the developer's assessment of the likely environmental effects of a proposed project and, if appropriate, what measures are envisaged to mitigate them. The European Directive on the Conservation of Natural Habitats and Wild Fauna and Flora (92/43/EEC) states that a coherent European ecological network be established under the title *Natura 2000* (European Union, 1992) to maintain or, where appropriate, restore (Brookes and Shields, 1996). This is promoting action outside strictly protected areas and the introduction of principles of sustainability for all forms of natural resource management (Stanners and Bordeau, 1995).

Points to consider and things to do

- What factors govern the amount of river channelisation that has taken place in different countries?

- Do you consider the level of expenditure on flood control measures for the Mississippi (and other rivers) to be justified? Explain your answer.

- List three major problems facing river managers.

- Is the creation of the Environment Agency for England and Wales and the Scottish Environment Protection Agency advantageous for river management in Great Britain? Support your argument.

2 Understanding the dynamics of river environments

- *What is the fluvial system?*

- *Why do river channels change their form?*

- *What are the main impacts of river flooding?*

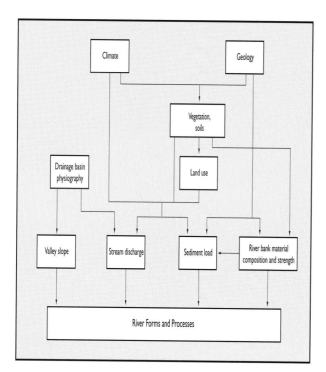

Figure 2.1 Interrelationships in the fluvial system
Source: adapted from Knighton, 1998, p. 2.

The term 'river environment' is used in this book to describe the river, any features within the river such as channel bars and river islands, the river channel banks and the adjoining floodplain. The river environment is an essential part of the fluvial system which is a highly interconnected system linking the processes in the river to those in the floodplain and wider river catchment (Figure 2.1). As highlighted by the Mississippi case study (see pp. 2–4), there are two key features of the river environment that require management: river channel adjustment and flooding. However, river environments are also ecosystems, and to manage them properly river managers need to understand both the physical processes and the related workings of river habitats.

2.1 The fluvial system

The fluvial system can be thought of as an open system with inflows and outflows of energy and matter (Knighton, 1984, p. 1). Inputs of energy

come in the form of solar radiation, inputs of matter in the form of precipitation, and outputs occur as evaporation and transpiration to the atmosphere combined with outflows of water and sediment at the mouth of the basin (Figure 2.2). Between the inputs and outputs, rivers act as the principal means of water and sediment transfer over the Earth's surface (Tables 2.1 and 2.2). Milliman and Meade (1983) estimate that the world's rivers deliver 13.5×10^9 tonnes of sediment to the oceans each year.

The character and behaviour of the fluvial system at any particular location reflects the combined effect of a number of controlling factors. Climate, geology, land use and basin shape are all major influences, and together they determine the river's hydrological regime and the quantity and type of sediment supply. Energy conditions within the system are also very important and may be influenced by base-level changes. For example, if a river drains into a lake, a falling lake level (base-level) can increase a river's potential energy and trigger upstream river bed erosion. In addition to these natural controls, the human influence is of major importance through changing patterns of

Table 2.1 **Largest rivers of the world in terms of discharge**

River	Discharge (10^3 m^3/s)
Amazon, Brazil	181.0
Congo, Congo	39.6
Orinoco, Venezuela	22.6
Yangtze, China	21.8
Brahmaputra, Bangladesh	20.0
Mississippi, United States	17.8
Yenisei, Soviet Union	17.4
Mekong, Thailand	15.0
Parana, Argentina	14.9
St Lawrence, Canada	14.1

Source: Morisawa, 1985, p. 12.
Note: the Amazon has a computed yearly discharge volume approximately one-fifth of the total discharge of all the rivers of the world.

Table 2.2   **Suspended load of some large river basins, ranked by tonnes/km^2**

River	Basin area (km^2)	Average annual suspended load (tonnes/km^2)
Yellow (Huang He), China	715	2913
Ganges, Bangladesh	1059	1544
Brahmaputra, Bangladesh	559	1428
Irrawaddy, Burma	368	903
Yangtze, China	1025	540
Indus, Pakistan	950	502
Mekong, Thailand	391	479
Colorado, USA	357	418
Missouri, USA	1368	175
Mississippi, USA	3222	107

Source: Morisawa, 1985, p. 13.

land use and, of course, river engineering. The construction of reservoirs, for instance, along river systems can change local base-levels and trigger erosion or sedimentation in this way.

The ecology of rivers is also determined by particular features of the fluvial system. There are obviously huge differences related to climate, but even within one climatic zone, river fauna and flora change in relation to controls such as geology and land use. Haslam and Wolseley (1981) provide a manual for river vegetation and its management and give details of the characteristic vegetation of a wide range of river habitats in Great Britain. River habitats are classified in terms of topography (plain, lowland, upland, mountain), rock type (chalk, limestone, clay, resistant rock, sandstone, alluvium) and stream size.

A comparison between typical lowland, medium streams (4 to 10 m wide and 30 to 75 cm deep) in chalk and resistant rock areas of Great Britain illustrates the influence of geology on river vegetation (Figure 2.3). While both river environments typically have six species of aquatic vegetation, the species are very different and the chalk stream supports a much more abundant vegetation cover.

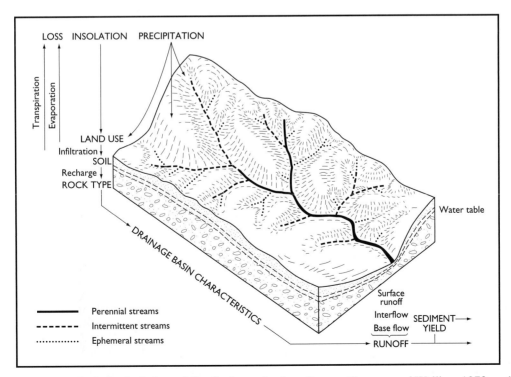

Figure 2.2   A geomorphological view of the drainage basin.   Source: Gregory and Walling, 1973, p. 10.

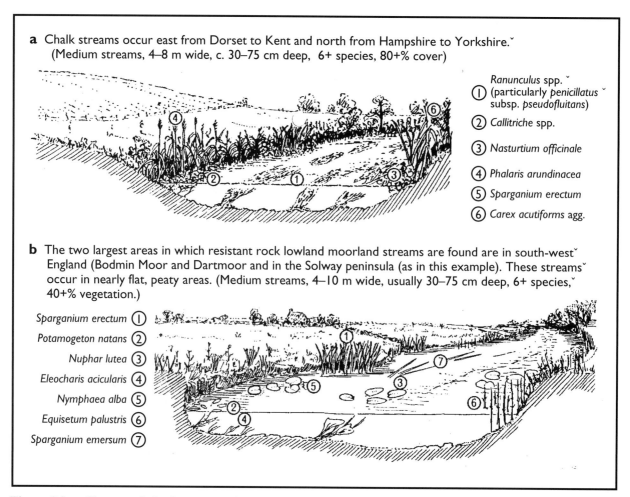

a Chalk streams occur east from Dorset to Kent and north from Hampshire to Yorkshire.ˇ
(Medium streams, 4–8 m wide, c. 30–75 cm deep, 6+ species, 80+% cover)

① *Ranunculus* spp. ˇ (particularly *penicillatus* ˇ subsp. *pseudofluitans*)

② *Callitriche* spp.

③ *Nasturtium officinale*

④ *Phalaris arundinacea*

⑤ *Sparganium erectum*

⑥ *Carex acutiforms* agg.

b The two largest areas in which resistant rock lowland moorland streams are found are in south-westˇ England (Bodmin Moor and Dartmoor and in the Solway peninsula (as in this example). These streamsˇ occur in nearly flat, peaty areas. (Medium streams, 4–10 m wide, usually 30–75 cm deep, 6+ species,ˇ 40+% vegetation.)

Sparganium erectum ①
Potamogeton natans ②
Nuphar lutea ③
Eleocharis acicularis ④
Nymphaea alba ⑤
Equisetum palustris ⑥
Sparganium emersum ⑦

Figure 2.3   Characteristic river vegetation   Source: P. A. Wolseley in Haslam and Wolseley, 1981, pp. 25 & 47.

2.2   River channel changes and river equilibrium

River channels are constantly changing their form and it is this dynamic behaviour that engineers have tried to control. Rivers can adjust to changes in catchment characteristics, such as deforestation, but it is the amount of water and sediment moving down a river that ultimately exerts the dominant control on channel form adjustment. In addition to these 'externally-imposed controls', feedback between river forms and processes can occur.

Such feedback is summarised in Figure 2.4, proposed by Ashworth and Ferguson (1986) after studying a braided stream in a glaciated catchment. The figure shows some of the key dynamic components in the river system. Entering the diagram at the top left, changing discharge through a river channel with a given topographic form and a given bed sedimentology, produces variable forces (shear stress) on the river bed, and variable flow velocities throughout the water column. These flow characteristics interact with the sediment on the river bed and the supply of sediment from upstream. This controls the sediment transport rate

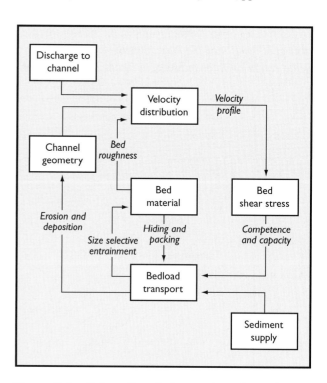

Figure 2.4   Interactions between river channel form, bed sedimentology, sediment transport and river channel change in a braided gravel-bed stream
Source: Ashworth and Ferguson, 1986.

and the patterns of erosion and deposition, which ultimately leads to a new channel geometry. Bedload transport itself feeds back upon the character of the bed material through the effects of selective transport. This results in changes to the bed topography since smaller particles are transported more easily and further, which further affects the water flow and sediment transport conditions in the river (Lane, 1995).

River channel adjustments can be described by considering the four principal components of river channel geometry which undergo changes (Figure 2.5). These are the river bed configuration (Figure 2.5a), the cross-sectional form (Figure 2.5b), the channel pattern (Figure 2.5c), and the channel bed slope and long profile (Figure 2.5d). These different features of the channel geometry can adjust over a range of spatial and temporal scales, as shown in Figure 2.6. River bed forms tend to be small-scale features which change quickly, such as during the passage of a single flood wave, in response to altered water or sediment discharges. Conversely, the long profile changes least of all, often adjusting over a time scale of thousands of years. It is also known that changes in the different components are frequently interlinked. For example, the development of a meandering channel pattern requires river bank erosion to take place (a change in cross-sectional form) and, in gravel-bed rivers, is also thought to be related to the formation of pool–riffle sequences (a bed configuration adjustment).

Figure 2.6, as well as describing the spatial and temporal scales of different channel form adjustments, also indicates how likely the different components are to change – that is, the *sensitivity* to channel change. Channel-bed form and cross-sectional form can change very rapidly, and they are regarded as highly adjustable or sensitive features of the physical river environment. In fact, channel width changes are some of the most widespread adjustments that river managers must contend with. The historic changes along the Cimmaron River in south-western Kansas, documented by Schumm and Lichty (1963), show just how sensitive channel width can be and how much adjustment is possible (see box).

Although rivers are dynamic, they also have an ability for self-regulation or negative feedback. This means that if they are disturbed they tend to return approximately to their previous state. *River stability* or *equilibrium* is reflected in the development of channel forms characteristic of

In 1874 the Cimmaron River ranged in width from 3 to 92 m and averaged 15.25 m in the six counties studied; it was narrow, meandering and stable, and the floodplain was grassed and provided good grazing. From 1914 until 1942, the channel widened until almost all of the floodplain was destroyed. The average channel widening over the period 1914 to 1939 was 350.6 m. After 1942 the channel became narrower again and averaged 176.8 m. From 1955 to 1969, it was mostly stable with some tendency to channel widening again.

Reasons for the channel changes on the Cimarron River
The behaviour of the Cimarron River was originally blamed on accelerated erosion caused by over-cultivation and the sequence of agricultural history. However, climatic fluctuations and vegetation were also shown to be important in controlling river processes. The period of channel widening accompanied a period of below-average precipitation but it was marked by floods of high peak discharge. The floods had a huge impact because the low average precipitation reduced the vegetation in the channel and lessened the protection against bank erosion. Conversely, in the wet years, a vigorous growth of perennial vegetation stabilised the existing river deposits and encouraged further deposition of sediment to promote floodplain construction.

Many more studies have since established that floods in semi-arid environments may be very destructive to the channel because of the absence of protective vegetation, and this knowledge has translated into the active use of vegetation to promote channel stability in all environments.

particular environments or physical conditions where controlling variables such as climate, geology, soils and vegetation are relatively constant. Thus, although braided river patterns occur in a wide range of environments, from proglacial to semi-arid, and at a large range of scales from the small streams on sandy beaches to the largest continental rivers, certain conditions seem to be conducive to their development. These

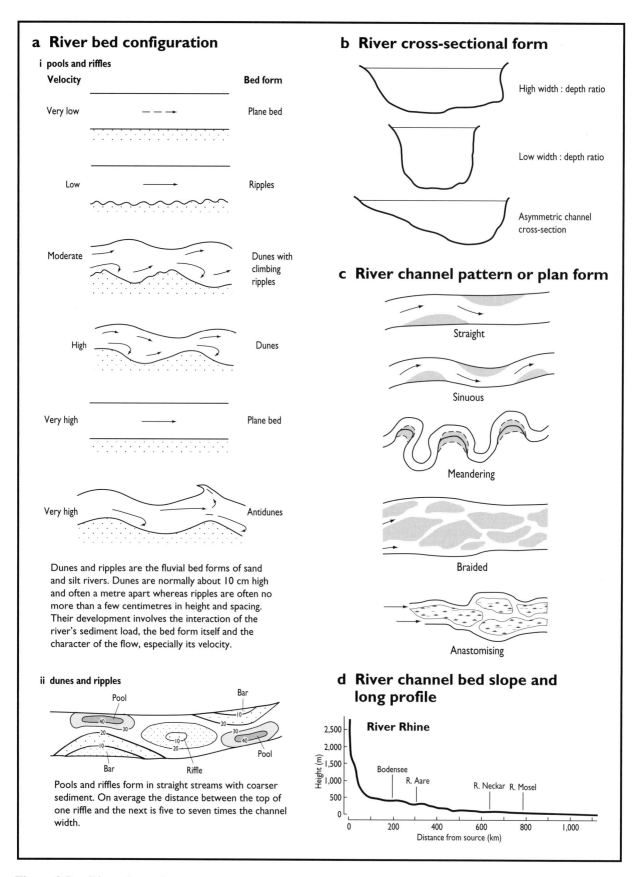

a River bed configuration

i pools and riffles

Velocity		Bed form
Very low		Plane bed
Low		Ripples
Moderate		Dunes with climbing ripples
High		Dunes
Very high		Plane bed
Very high		Antidunes

Dunes and ripples are the fluvial bed forms of sand and silt rivers. Dunes are normally about 10 cm high and often a metre apart whereas ripples are often no more than a few centimetres in height and spacing. Their development involves the interaction of the river's sediment load, the bed form itself and the character of the flow, especially its velocity.

ii dunes and ripples

Pool   Bar

Bar   Riffle   Pool

Pools and riffles form in straight streams with coarser sediment. On average the distance between the top of one riffle and the next is five to seven times the channel width.

b River cross-sectional form

High width : depth ratio

Low width : depth ratio

Asymmetric channel cross-section

c River channel pattern or plan form

Straight

Sinuous

Meandering

Braided

Anastomising

d River channel bed slope and long profile

River Rhine

Height (m): 2,500 · 2,000 · 1,500 · 1,000 · 500 · 0

Bodensee   R. Aare   R. Neckar R. Mosel

Distance from source (km): 0 · 200 · 400 · 600 · 800 · 1,000

Figure 2.5   River channel geometry
(a) bed configuration: (i) pools and riffles (ii) dunes and ripples
(Source: Briggs and Smithson, 1985, p. 343)
(b) cross-sectional form
(c) channel pattern types (Source: Morisawa, 1985, p. 90)
(d) long profile (Source: Knighton, 1984, p. 149).

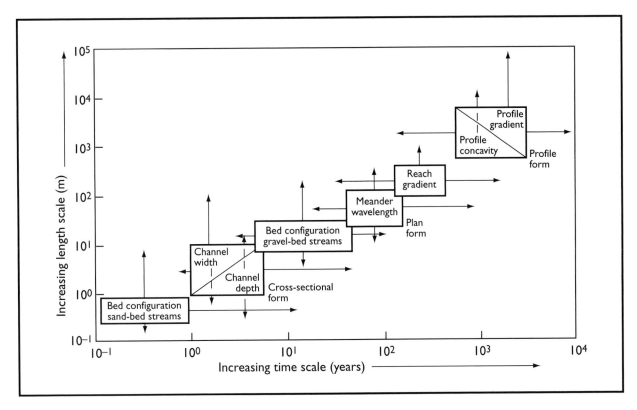

Figure 2.6   Adjustment of river channel form over a range of spatial and temporal scales
Source: Knighton, 1998, p. 158.

include an abundant bed load, erodible river banks, a highly variable discharge and steep slopes to provide the energy for bank erosion.

Channel adjustments typically occur around these average or *characteristic forms* (Figure 2.7). Steady state equilibrium reflects a situation in which there is an absence of channel change over the time span of 10 to 100 years. Dynamic equilibrium reflects a situation in which a short-term balance between river channel geometry and the controlling variables is achieved but where changes in the river form take place in the longer term. One possible scenario would be change to a wetter climate resulting in larger floods and river channel widening through increased bank erosion. The oscillations that take place in dynamic equilibrium may be greater than changes in the trend itself so that when a system is observed over a short time-period it gives an impression of steady state equilibrium. This tendency towards a steady state is termed quasi-equilibrium (Knighton, 1984)

Early attempts at designing stable river channels tried, unrealistically, to impose a static equilibrium on the river. To try to prevent all channel adjustments, rivers were encased in rigid, resistant linings such as concrete, but this has had unexpected and expensive consequences, as we will discover in Chapter 4.

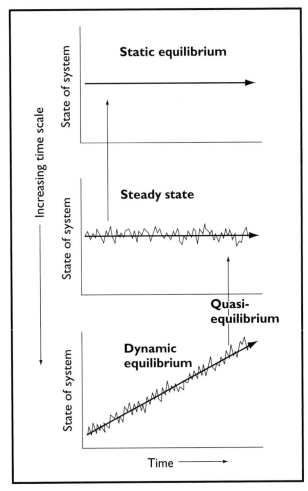

Figure 2.7   Types of river channel equilibrium
Source: Knighton, 1984, p. 91.

2.3 Floods and their impacts

In addition to the task of managing river channel changes there is the related, and equally difficult, task of managing river floods. Large floods are normally the cause of major river channel adjustments.

Floods are repeatedly in the headlines of the local, national and international media and, of all natural phenomena, flooding affects the greatest number of people. Deaths from flooding worldwide, over the quarter-century ending in 1990, exceeded 100,000, but as many as three-quarters of a billion people were distressed or disrupted by flooding in some way. And, in an examination of the major natural disasters in 1990, Berz (1992) showed that floods accounted for 123 of the 420 events (29 per cent of the total) and resulted in 2,535 deaths (5 per cent) and US$ 4200 million (9 per cent) economic loss.

Defining a flood is difficult. For most practical purposes a meaningful definition will incorporate the notions of damage and inundation. Here are three popular definitions from Ward's (1978, pp. 4–5) book on floods:

- *A flood is a relatively high flow that overtaxes the natural channel provided for the runoff.*

- *A flood is any high streamflow that overtops natural or artificial banks of a stream.* [This definition covers the many engineered rivers in the world.]

- *A flood is a body of water that rises to overflow land that is not normally submerged.* [In this definition, inundation is explicit and damage is implied in the final three words.]

Many factors determine the nature and severity of flood impacts, such as the depth and area of inundation, the duration of the flood and the velocity of the floodwaters. For example, a depth of inundation of about one metre, with a velocity of $1 \, m \, s^{-1}$ could cause widespread structural damage and even loss of life, while an inundation depth of 3 m will result in damage to the contents of buildings above ground-level.

2.3.1 Examples of devastating flood events

The 1998 summer floods in Bangladesh were the worst on record this century. Heavier than normal monsoon rains, a disruption to the regional weather patterns by the El Niño effect, and cyclones combined with snowmelt from the Himalayas, caused the Brahmaputra, Ganges and Meghna rivers to reach flood levels at the same time, with devastating consequences (Figure 2.8). By 5 October 1998, 1,500 deaths had been recorded and it was estimated that out of a total population of 124 million, approximately 35 million had been made homeless by the floods (http://www.independent-bangladesh.com/news; http://www.whoban.org/floods).

At the height of the flood, over two-thirds of the country (1 million km^2) was submerged, including 750 million hectares of agricultural land. Most of the country's autumn rice crop was destroyed and total crop losses have been estimated at US$ 300 million. Other damages included flooding of 10,000 km of roads and 4,200 km of embankments. The cost of rebuilding the embankments alone is estimated at US$ 127.65 million (http://www.telegraph.co.uk; http://www.guardian.co.uk/archive.html).

In the summer of 1993, flooding of the Mississippi River brought chaos to the American Mid-West. More than 100 rivers overtopped their banks, 14 rivers reached their highest levels ever and the flood area was 1,290 km long and 800 km wide at its broadest point. The flood disaster claimed 48 lives and left 70,000 people homeless (Table 2.3).

Some of the most serious floods recently experienced in Western Europe were those that occurred between December 1993 and January 1994. In England and Wales the then National Rivers Authority issued 155 flood alerts as rivers across the whole of southern England, as well as many in South Wales and parts of Northern Ireland, flooded. The cost of flooding in southern England was estimated at £100 million. Floods also ravaged The Netherlands, Belgium, Germany and France, and thousands were evacuated from their homes, including 8,000 people in northern France. In Germany five people lost their lives, and the Dutch Government declared the floods a national disaster.

In July and August 1997, central Europe experienced its worst floods this century. Flooding was focused along the Oder and Neisse Rivers, which affected eastern Germany, Poland, the Czech Republic and Romania. In Frankfurt an der Oder, which is situated just downstream of the confluence of the River Neisse with the River Oder, the waters were 1 cm above the level of the record level of 1930 and reached the highest level

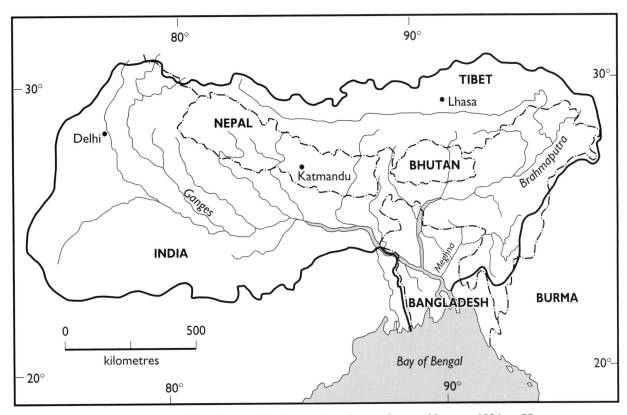

Figure 2.8   Catchment area of the Ganges / Brahmaputra rivers   Source: Newson, 1994, p. 88.

since records began in the eighteenth century. It is estimated that 128 people were killed in the 1997 central European floods, including at least 60 people in Poland and at least 46 people in the Czech Republic. In Poland, 140,000 people were evacuated with 62,000 left homeless. The homeless figure in the Czech Republic was reported at 10,000. Hundreds of thousands of hectares of crops were destroyed across central Europe resulting in a total flood damage estimate of about £4 billion for Poland and the Czech Republic.

The floods were caused by high rainfall totals resulting from a persistent low pressure system over central Europe in July 1997 which yielded steady rainfall for over one week and two periods of heavy convectional rainfall superimposed on this. The first period of intense convectional rainfall occurred in early July (6–9 July) and the second between one and two weeks later, depending on geographical location. The July rainfall figures (supplied by the Met Office) for Lysa Hora in the Czech Republic (49° 36' N,

Table 2.3   **Impact of the 1993 Mississippi flood**

State	Flood deaths	Property damage (US$ million)	Agricultural loss (US$ million)	Number of counties receiving disaster assistance
Minnesota	4	51.3	740–990	46
North Dakota	2	100	420	37
South Dakota	3	25.7	725	37
Iowa	5	1250	450	99 (all)
Nebraska	2	50	292	51
Illinois	4	930	565	30
Missouri	25	2000	2000	76
Kansas	1	160	434.4	43
Wisconsin	2	101	800	45

Source: Goldstein and Haynes, 1993.

18° 30' E) illustrate the extreme nature of the rainfall event in central Europe. Between 6 and 9 July 1997 over 1,000 mm of rain fell at Lysa Hora, and on 7 July 1997 a staggering 333.8 mm of rainfall was recorded. The total rainfall figure for July was 1,471.9 mm, compared with a usual monthly average of 200 mm.

Although extreme rainfall was the primary cause of the central European floods, the impacts were undoubtedly worsened locally by breaches in dykes. For example, on 25 July 1997 the River Oder burst through a dyke on its west bank at Beeskow-Finkenheerd, a few kilometres south of Frankfurt an der Oder. The hole rapidly widened to 250 m and water flowed at a rate of 500 m^3 s^{-1} into a surrounding low-lying area measuring 60 km^2. Poor co-operation over the opening of floodgates and the timing of releases from reservoirs also exacerbated the situation and created cross-border tensions between Poland and the Czech Republic and Poland and eastern Germany. For example, rescue workers in Frankfurt an der Oder were not notified by Poland of a decision to empty reservoirs into the river, causing a surge in river levels. Germany also criticised the under-investment in the infrastructure of the dykes by its poorer neighbours.

Associated impacts included water pollution problems and the threat of disease and a serious financial situation. Most of the 45,000 Poles whose households were destroyed were not insured against natural disasters. However, Polish and Czech victims received EU aid worth about £1.6 million, and Poland received UN emergency assistance. On 23 July 1997 the German Cabinet approved £6.6 million of emergency assistance to flood victims in eastern Germany and a promise of talks about special tax relief. The Kreditanstalt für Wiederaufbau, the state-owned development bank, also announced that it would provide £66 million in credits at half the market interest rate to cover damages.

The floods also re-opened the debate on the development of floodplain wetlands. In Germany the floods prompted complaints about recent decisions to build an aluminium smelting plant in the Saarland (destroying vital marshland needed for drainage) and planned new building projects along the River Elbe.

Strictly speaking, though, floods are not natural disasters. Floods are natural phenomena and form part of the normally occurring range of streamflow conditions (just as does drought at the other end of the scale). Yearly floods are necessary to maintain the fertility of the floodplains. For example, the 'barsha' flood events in Bangladesh cover the land with nutrient-rich alluvial sediment. However, the low-frequency floods which occur (such as the July 1998 flood), known as 'banna' floods, cause widespread loss of life and damage to the nation's economy. Since stream channels can carry only a fraction of peak flood flows, part of the excess must flow through and over, or be stored on, the floodplain. In flood conditions, therefore, channels and their adjacent floodplains together form the means by which floodwaters are transmitted. Flood disasters are therefore human-made in that people have put themselves at risk by developing floodplains for settlement, agriculture and industry and by building roads, bridges and railway lines in floodable positions. Such intrusions into the floodway may result from ignorance or for economic reasons (that is, the risk is worth taking or worth safeguarding against) or from lack of choice. In Bangladesh, 80 per cent of the country is floodplain and this land must of necessity be settled and farmed; in the USA 10 million Americans live in significantly defined floodplains and another 25 million where they could be affected by floods (American Water Resources Association, 1972); and nearly half the population of the Far East continually faces the danger of floods.

These recent examples illustrate some of the dramatic consequences of floods and how the impact of flooding differs according to a country's level of development. In the less developed world, flood events tragically claim thousands of lives each year, whereas in developed countries the cost of structural damage caused by floods is enormous but human casualties are usually much lower.

2.3.2 Frequency of flooding

To aid the management of flooding, it is important to have some knowledge about how often floods will occur (flood frequency) and how quickly rivers will flood following the onset of rainfall (lag times). Large rivers that normally show very marked seasonal characteristics tend to attain their peak flow in the wet season. On smaller streams, however, the most severe flooding may be associated with intense convectional storms in summer, such as the 1952 flood at Lynmouth, Devon. In August 1952, 20 million m^3 litres of water fell over the 100 km^2 Exmoor catchment and the discharge reached 511 m^3 s^{-1}, a figure only twice exceeded by the River Thames this century in a basin 100 times larger. In total, about 100,000 tons of boulders were moved onto the lower Lyn valley (Hilton, 1979, p. 83).

Clearly, where flooding has a marked and reliable seasonal character, adaptation to the flood hazard is easier. But floods may occur at any time of the year. *Flood frequency* is a statistical measure of the probable occurrence of a flood of a given size and is used by hydrologists in predicting floods. Large floods occur relatively infrequently – they have large *return periods* or *recurrence intervals* of perhaps several hundreds of years – while small floods occur frequently, perhaps two or three times a year, and therefore have a very low return period or recurrence interval. The one-year flood and the 1,000-year flood can occur at any time, but naturally the one-year flood is more likely. This has important implications for the way floodplains are developed, since the only floods likely to have been experienced are the more frequent minor ones whose impact is comparatively small.

The statistical likelihood of a given flood occurrence provides important evidence for hydrologists and engineers. However, the average floodplain occupant warned of an imminent flood event will be more concerned with the time left to evacuate family and possessions to higher ground. To provide this information a *flood hydrograph* is used (Figure 2.9) which is a continuous plot of discharge against time during a flood event.

Through detailed and regular flow measurements along individual rivers at river gauging stations it is possible for hydrologists to construct characteristic flood hydrographs for individual rivers. These can then be used to forecast the likely response of future flood events so that flood warnings can be given.

The average time between a rainstorm or snowmelt event and the resulting increase in streamflow is referred to as the *lag time*, or basin lag, or time to rise. Lag may be measured in a number of ways, and two important measures are shown in Figure 2.9. These are the time from the rainfall peak to the discharge peak (T_1) and the time from the attainment of actual flood conditions, for example bankfull discharge, to the peak discharge (T_2). The second interval may be considerably shorter than the first and in socio-economic terms is normally the more important. This is because people generally do not become concerned with flooding until actual flood conditions have been reached, so that the period T_2 represents the time available for adjusting to the oncoming flood.

Flood prediction and flood forecasting are greatly aided when long-term, accurate discharge records are available for rivers. Sadly, many rivers are without river gauging stations, particularly in less developed countries. For such situations, hydrologists have devised techniques that allow flood information to be derived from a knowledge of catchment characteristics and the runoff process.

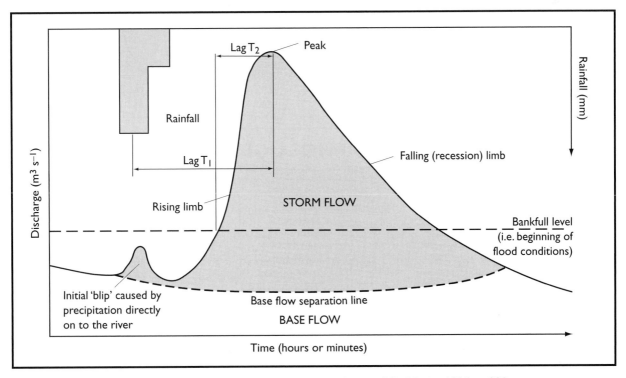

Figure 2.9   The flood hydrograph Source: adapted from Briggs and Smithson, 1985, p. 220.

22

In Britain the *Flood Studies Report* (NERC, 1975) contained the first comprehensive set of instructions for estimating floods using these 'indirect' techniques, and these procedures are now used widely by hydrologists. An updated version, the *Flood Estimation Handbook*, was published in 1999 (Reed, 1999).

A similar indirect technique uses relationships between river channel size and discharge to estimate flood magnitudes and frequency (Hedman and Osterkamp, 1982; Wharton, 1995). These channel-geometry equations have developed from the knowledge that river channel dimensions are adjusted over time to the amount of water and sediment coming down the river. The equations have yielded reliable indirect flood estimates in a large number of river environments worldwide.

In addition to the human impact of flooding, river managers must also understand the geomorphic effectiveness of floods. The geomorphic work accomplished by a flood can be measured in terms of the amount of sediment transported by the flood or the degree of river channel adjustment which takes place during flooding.

The debate over which floods perform most 'work' has continued for some time. Although large catastrophic events appear impressive, it is now accepted by geomorphologists that, over time, and in many environments, most work is carried out by events of moderate magnitude which recur relatively frequently rather than by rare events of unusual magnitude. There are exceptions though. For example, dramatic channel changes in response to single floods, or sets of floods, have

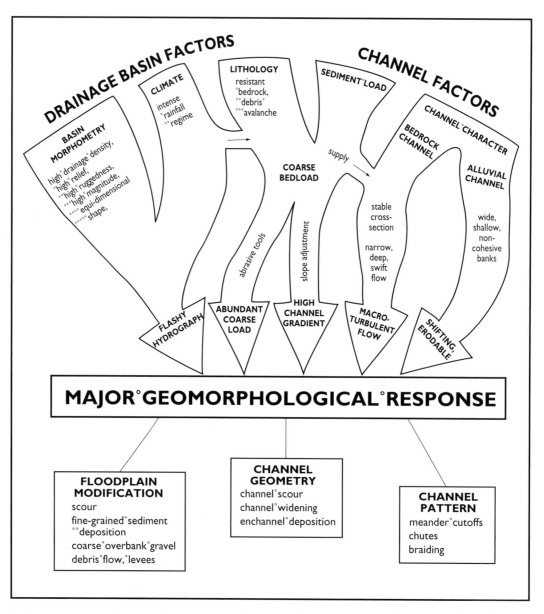

Figure 2.10 **Summary schematic diagram of the factors important in controlling channel and floodplain response to large-magnitude floods** Source: Kochel, 1988, p. 184.

been reported in semi-arid environments (e.g. Schumm and Lichty, 1963; Burkham, 1972; Baker, 1977) and rivers in semi-arid areas appear more prone to the long-lasting impact of high-magnitude events than rivers in more humid areas. Rivers in arid and semi-arid environments are said to have a longer 'memory' for flood events. The influence of extreme events (Figure 2.10) is also greater in smaller catchments because of their more flashy hydrological regime (Wolman and Gerson, 1978).

2.4   Conclusions: the need for river management

'Unless we have control of the floods, we cannot feed the people. Unless the people are fed, how can they read or write anything? We have to bring the vast majority of the population to acceptable economic standards. Eighty per cent of the population are dependent on agriculture in this country, more than 60 per cent of the population are below subsistence level. Now who is saying: live with floods?'
(Komol Siddiqi, Flood Plan Co-ordination Organisation, Bangladesh, speaking in 1994 on the BBC Horizon programme 'After the Flood')

All countries are dependent on river environments, some to a huge extent, and managing floods and river channel changes is therefore essential to economic development. In Bangladesh, for example, floods are its single biggest problem but they are also its lifeline. Rivers are natural mechanisms for the transport of water and sediment through drainage basins, and river floods bring much-needed water, sediment and nutrients to floodplains and wetlands to replenish soil moisture and soil fertility.

The dwellers of floodplain wetlands in West Africa, such as the Hadejia-Jam'are floodplain in Nigeria, also rely on annual floods to sustain their indigenous way of life which is based on a carefully planned mix of floodwater cropping, grazing and fishing. They have developed farming practices to minimise the flood hazard, and the floodplains yield a rich harvest.

These two examples, however, indicate the importance of making a distinction between 'normal' flooding to which farming practices are well adapted, and 'damaging' floods which occur when water rises earlier, higher, more rapidly or later than farmers expect. This is when floods become hazardous and it is against such a hazard that flood protection is necessary.

In more developed countries, with a long history of river engineering, a further dilemma needs to be addressed. There is clear evidence that the flood situation is getting worse in terms of the increasing damage caused by flooding. Expenditure on flood defences is related to the risk of flooding but this risk is often most easily reduced by not building within the floodplain in the first place. There is also increasing evidence that protective measures may actually be counter-productive since by encouraging greater development on floodplains and engendering a false sense of security they may result in even higher damages than would otherwise have occurred.

That river environments need to be managed is clear; it is how this is achieved that is critical. River managers are learning from the mistakes of past decades and are beginning to demonstrate how the management of floods and river channel change can be achieved in a sensitive and sustainable way.

Points to consider and things to do

- Refer to a geological map of Great Britain to identify the areas of chalk and resistant rocks. Name at least one lowland chalk stream. Name at least one upland resistant rock stream.

- List all the physical and human impacts of flooding you can think of.

- Describe the benefits of river flooding.

- What is the main problem with the concept of a return period or recurrence interval in describing the threat of flooding?

- If you have access to the Internet World Wide Web, why not take a look at the articles published during July and August 1997 as the floods were happening in central Europe. As a start, look up the articles published in *The Times* (http://www.the-times.co.uk). Try a search for all articles published between 20 July and 10 August 1997, using the key words 'River Oder' for your search. Some other useful Internet site addresses are:
  Financial Times: http://www.FT.com
  Daily Telegraph: http://www.telegraph.co.uk
  and
  The Independent: http://www.independent.co.uk

3 Traditional engineering approaches to river management

- *What are the main engineering techniques traditionally used to control river floods and river channel adjustments?*

- *Can floods and river channel changes ever be fully controlled?*

A large number of engineering techniques have been developed to modify river channels for flood and erosion control and these are known collectively as *channelisation*. The techniques include: increasing the width and/or the depth of the channel to increase its ability to transport flood flows (resectioning); steepening the river's gradient through channel straightening to increase the velocity of the water (realignment); confining floodwaters by raising the height of channel banks (embanking or levee construction); using structures to prevent river bank erosion (bank protection); and removing obstacles in the river to increase the speed of water flow (clearing and snagging).

Some of these engineering techniques are used primarily to alleviate flooding, whereas others focus on controlling river channel adjustment, although in many situations it is usually necessary to address the problems of flooding and erosion together using a combination of techniques. Thus many river channelisation projects are *comprehensive* or *composite* in nature.

3.1 Managing river floods

Flood management aims to prevent flood discharges overtopping the channel banks and spilling out onto the surrounding floodplain. Nearly 5,000 km^2 of land in England and Wales are below sea-level and are protected from inundation by a range of structural flood defences. The task is to design and construct a river that will contain and transmit floods of specified sizes.

3.1.1 The design flood

To design a suitable channel, information is needed on the sizes of floods experienced along the river and how often these floods are likely to occur. Information on flood magnitude and frequency normally comes from a study of the river's historical flood records and a set of calculations

known as *flood frequency analysis*. We know from experience that large flood events are quite rare whereas smaller floods occur more often. This frequency of occurrence is expressed in terms of a *return period* or *recurrence interval*, measured in years. The flood discharge commonly used in river engineering design is the 100-year flood. This the flood that is equalled or exceeded once every 100 years *on average*. The return period provides a measure of the likelihood or probability of a specified flood event occurring. The important point to remember is that the return period does not tell us *when* the flood will occur. Thus the 100-year flood could occur on the river tomorrow, in 10 years' time or 50 years' time, but *on average it will be experienced once every 100 years*. A central problem in flood management is that the natural river channel is adjusted to cope with floods that have a natural recurrence interval of 1–2 years, but to protect developments on the floodplain, structures are built to try to contain the 100-year flood event.

The flood discharge, with its associated magnitude and frequency, selected for use in a river engineering project is known as the *design discharge* or *design flood*. River channel dimensions are calculated to carry all floods up to this size. Computer models allow engineers to check these calculations before construction begins by showing how the design flood flows along the proposed river channel. The computer models are known as *flow routeing models*.

The design discharge is selected to reflect the level of protection required. A commonly held view is that where human life is at risk, structures should be designed to cope with the *probable maximum flood* (PMF) without risk of failure. The PMF is defined as a flood that can be expected from the worst combination of meteorological and hydrological conditions possible. But this represents an extreme situation against which it is seldom feasible to provide complete protection, mainly for economic reasons. The judgement and experience of hydrologists and engineers tends to play a dominant part in the selection of a design flood, and in the USA two other design floods are widely adopted. The *intermediate regional flood* is defined as a major flood having a minimum average recurrence rate of 100 years at a particular location. The *standard project flood* represents the flood that would be rarely exceeded and, although assigned no specific frequency, it is a useful design standard providing a high degree of protection. It is defined as a flood that can be expected from the most severe combination of meteorological and hydrological conditions characteristic of the geographical area in which the drainage basin is located, and is a more realistic flood to provide protection against than the PMF (Ward, 1978, pp. 68–71).

3.1.2 Resectioning

Resectioning is the method of enlarging river channels by widening and/or deepening them (Plate 3.1). The aim is to increase the cross-sectional area of the channel so that flood flows that would have previously spread onto the floodplain are contained. The result of channel enlargement is that a given quantity of water flows through the river channel at a lower and, therefore, safer level. Resectioning may be necessary downstream of storm-water outfalls in urban areas

Plate 3.1   Newly-resectioned channel, Lake District, UK.

Plate 3.2   Rectangular concrete channel, Lloret de Mar, Spain.

or downstream of drainage outfalls from agricultural land if the river is to cope with the increased runoff. Deepening of the river channel through excavation of the river bed may also be undertaken to lower the water-table in the adjacent floodplain as part of a land drainage operation.

Resectioned channels typically have three channel shapes. Trapezoidal cross-sections are often designed for river channels with unlined earth banks to provide sloping sides for stability (Plate 3.1); rectangular cross-sections are used for channels built of stable materials such as concrete (Plate 3.2); and triangular sections are used for small drainage ditches and roadside gutters.

Resectioning is usually combined with a process known as *regrading*. This comprises smoothing out the river channel bed, by removing features such as riffles and pools and depositional bars, to allow the water to flow more easily.

3.1.3 Embanking or levee construction

Embankments, also known as levees, flood banks and stopbanks, are one of the oldest forms of flood protection and they are used in both rural and urban areas provided there is sufficient land for construction (Figure 3.1). Like resectioning, the aim is to increase the capacity of the river channel to prevent flood flows spreading out onto the floodplain. Embankments, normally built of earth and clay, can be placed immediately adjacent to the river if building land is in short supply, or just outside the meander belt of a migrating river to avoid erosion if more land is available. Thus the alignment of embankments is affected by the topography of the floodplain and the human infrastructure.

Embankments are key components in the flood control systems along the lower courses of large

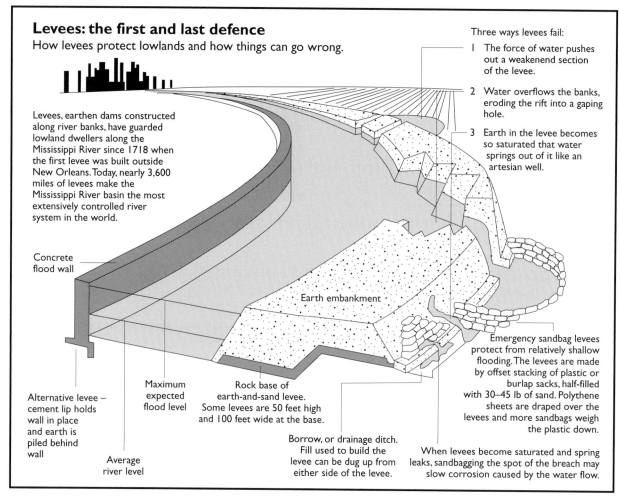

Levees: the first and last defence
How levees protect lowlands and how things can go wrong.

Three ways levees fail:

1 The force of water pushes out a weakenend section of the levee.

2 Water overflows the banks, eroding the rift into a gaping hole.

3 Earth in the levee becomes so saturated that water springs out of it like an artesian well.

Levees, earthen dams constructed along river banks, have guarded lowland dwellers along the Mississippi River since 1718 when the first levee was built outside New Orleans. Today, nearly 3,600 miles of levees make the Mississippi River basin the most extensively controlled river system in the world.

Concrete flood wall

Earth embankment

Emergency sandbag levees protect from relatively shallow flooding. The levees are made by offset stacking of plastic or burlap sacks, half-filled with 30–45 lb of sand. Polythene sheets are draped over the levees and more sandbags weigh the plastic down.

Alternative levee – cement lip holds wall in place and earth is piled behind wall

Maximum expected flood level

Rock base of earth-and-sand levee. Some levees are 50 feet high and 100 feet wide at the base.

Average river level

Borrow, or drainage ditch. Fill used to build the levee can be dug up from either side of the levee.

When levees become saturated and spring leaks, sandbagging the spot of the breach may slow corrosion caused by the water flow.

Figure 3.1 Cross-section through an embankment Source: Goldstein and Haynes (eds), 1993, p. 24.

rivers such as the Mississippi, Missouri and Sacramento Rivers in the USA where they protect major towns and cities which have become established on wide floodplains. There are also over 1,000 km of embankments alongside the Nile, 1,400 km alongside the Red River in Vietnam, and 700 km along the Yellow River (Huang He) in China.

The design specifications for embankments are very detailed, although the main considerations (for example Table 3.1) relate to the elevation, side slopes and construction materials. The elevation of an embankment is determined by the design discharge after computer tests have shown that the structure can contain this high flow. However, an embankment should not be built too high because of the increased danger to the population if the bank were to be overtopped or breached during an extreme flow event. Catastrophic flooding along the Mississippi River in 1993 demonstrated how flood damage can occur when embankments are breached.

The embankment slopes must not be over-steep, otherwise failure may occur. Trapezoidal sections typically have 1:2 side slopes but in rural areas

side slope gradients are usually less steep at 1:7. The top of the embankment should also be at least 2 m wide to allow access to maintenance traffic, and berms may be incorporated between the natural channel and the foot of the structure to further increase the discharge capacity of the engineered channel and allow improved access for maintenance (Figure 3.1).

Embankments are normally constructed from material excavated from the channel or a borrow pit in the floodplain. Sometimes imported materials are necessary and rubble and clay, shingle, and sands and clays may be used. New banks require a site investigation to determine information on the soil type and properties, particularly the engineering strength of the soil. Low-strength soils will limit the height of the embankment or may necessitate importing stronger building materials. Older embankments often require extensive maintenance, including strengthening with willow poles and steel sheets, and dredging of the channel is periodically required to remove silt that would formerly have been an overbank deposit at times of high flow.

Table 3.1   **Design considerations for stopbanks (embankments) in New Zealand**

1 Establish the justification for stopbanks. This is determined by the width of the valley floor, its present and potential condition; the width of the flood channel required to take the design flood; and the relationship of benefits and costs.	designed to withstand overtopping, or floodways/spillways may be constructed to carry flows at high flood stages.
2 Do not locate too close to an eroding river bank, and avoid unstable ground. The width between banks should not be confined to such a degree that flood levels are raised to a dangerously high level. On braided rivers the location of stopbanks on river terraces often has considerable advantages.	4 Check foundations, especially where the stopbank crosses a peat swamp or an old river channel. 5 Bank section depends on flood characteristics of the river, the type of material and construction methods. Preferred section for low to medium banks is 2 m top width and 2:1 side slopes. Provision of clay blanket is desirable.
3 Where a high degree of protection is required, banks are designed to the 25–100 years' flood standard, with 0.6–1.0 m freeboard depending on the characteristics of the river and the exposure of the bank to direct attack or wave action. Where a low to moderate standard of protection is required then the banks may be	6 Key the bank into the foundations; satisfactory compaction of material is essential. 7 Grazing of banks is necessary to limit growth of vegetation, and controlled grazing is desirable.

Source: Brookes, 1988, p. 32 (after Acheson, 1968).

3.1.4 Lined channels

Channels fully-lined with protective artificial materials are frequently constructed in urban areas where space for embankments is limited and access for maintenance restricted (Plate 3.2). Lined channels are normally rectangular in shape, with a horizontal bed and vertical sides. Straightening of the channel is also common. The channels may be constructed from reinforced or mass concrete or steel sheeting, and steel sheets may be faced with brick or stone to improve the visual appearance. Lined channels are used for flood control because the smooth channel boundary reduces the channel roughness. The reduced friction between the channel bed and banks and the streamflow increases the water velocity and decreases the water level for a given discharge. The overall result is an increase in the channel's carrying capacity. Channel size is again determined by the design flood, and the channel gradient is designed to prevent sediment deposition.

3.1.5 Realignment or straightening

These methods aim to improve the ease with which water flows through a river reach. Removing obstacles within the channel increases water flow velocities and reduces flood levels. The techniques range from removing sediment deposits (shoals) in the river by dredging to the complete removal of meander bends through cutoff programmes to achieve channel straightening.

'Rock-raking' is practised on gravel-bed rivers in New Zealand whereby the heavier material in the shoals is loosened and removed. This removal of boulders, sometimes up to 4 tonnes in weight, also helps to reduce the damage caused to bridges by moving sediment.

Straightening through cutoffs reduces the flood height by increasing the river gradient and therefore the flow velocity (see Figure 1.1). Cutoff programmes have been widely used on some of the world's largest rivers such as the Middle Yangtze, the Yellow River (Huang He) and the Lower Mississippi, where channel straightening also improves manoeuvrability for river traffic. Highway construction may also require channel realignment, for example the channel straightening that took place on the River Wylye near Stapleford, Wiltshire, in 1982 to facilitate road widening.

28

3.1.6 Diversion channels

These are relief channels, constructed to divert flood flows from an area requiring protection while the natural channel continues to carry the normal flows. Diversion channels are favoured in urban areas where it is not possible to widen the existing channel due the density of development. Cutoff channels can be used as an entirely separate river system to divert all flow away from an area. The Great Ouse Flood Protection Scheme, for example, relies on the flow of the Rivers Lark, Little Ouse and Wissey being directed along a 43 km cutoff channel from Mildenhall to Denver Sluice. A new flood alleviation scheme for Maidenhead, Windsor and Eton also relies on the construction of a 'by-pass' channel (Figure 3.2).

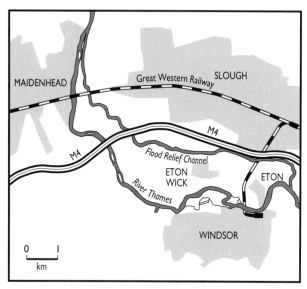

Figure 3.2   Alignment of the Maidenhead, Windsor and Eton flood alleviation scheme
Source: British Hydrological Society, 1994, p. 3.

In New Zealand, 'floodways' are used to provide a means of diverting water across the neck of a meander or a series of meanders to speed the transmission of the flood flows. An inlet to a floodway may be controlled and only opened during flood events.

Most importantly, diversion channels need to be sufficiently large to cope with flood flows and to be effective in reducing the height of the flood wave. This requires that the point of return of the floodwaters is sufficiently far downstream to allow the floodwaters to dissipate safely.

3.1.7 Culverts

As towns and cities developed, many watercourses were culverted with masonry arches or encased in

Plate 3.3   Culverted stream – Lloret de Mar.

large-diameter concrete or metal pipes (Plate 3.3). Streams in London, including the River Fleet, have become buried in culverts beneath the streets; the River Westbourne, for example, flows in an iron pipe above the platform at Sloane Square underground station.

The size of a culvert is determined by the design flood, and the risk of this flood being exceeded is a major problem. The flooding in Chichester in January 1994 was part of the widespread flooding experienced across the whole of southern England at that time. However, the culvert, which normally carries the River Lavant under the town to the sea, proved inadequate to cope with a streamflow four times the normal level, resulting in extensive flooding in the Hornet area of the town (Figure 3.3). Not surprisingly, the culverting of streams in urban areas of New Zealand, which are subject to particularly severe flash flooding, is not recommended because of the risk to life and property.

Problems of access for maintenance means that debris may build up inside culverts and reduce their capacity to dangerous levels. In a series of small coastal towns on the Costa Brava, Spain, tourists parking their cars at the entrance of culverts in ephemeral streams cause a major hazard

Plate 3.4   Large culvert and cars on an ephemeral stream (Arenys de Munt, Spain).

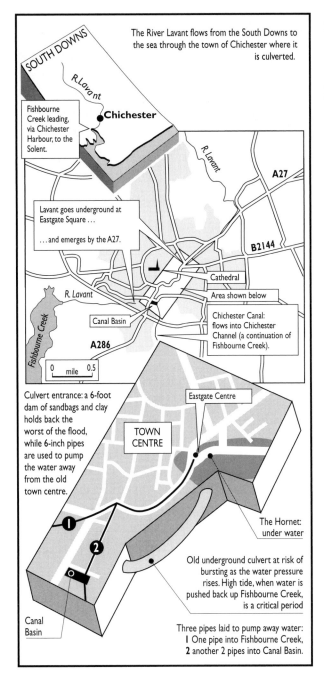

The River Lavant flows from the South Downs to the sea through the town of Chichester where it is culverted.

SOUTH DOWNS

R. Lavant

Chichester

Fishbourne Creek leading, via Chichester Harbour, to the Solent.

R. Lavant

A27

Lavant goes underground at Eastgate Square ...

... and emerges by the A27.

B2144

Cathedral

R. Lavant

Area shown below

Canal Basin

Chichester Canal: flows into Chichester Channel (a continuation of Fishbourne Creek).

A286

Fishbourne Creek

0   mile   0.5

Culvert entrance: a 6-foot dam of sandbags and clay holds back the worst of the flood, while 6-inch pipes are used to pump the water away from the old town centre.

Eastgate Centre

TOWN CENTRE

❶

❷

Canal Basin

The Hornet: under water

Old underground culvert at risk of bursting as the water pressure rises. High tide, when water is pushed back up Fishbourne Creek, is a critical period

Three pipes laid to pump away water:
1 One pipe into Fishbourne Creek,
2 another 2 pipes into Canal Basin.

Figure 3.3 Map of the Chichester culvert and the 1994 flood area
Source: *The Guardian*, 11 January 1994, p. 18.

as the flash floodwaters are forced to find alternative routes – normally along the town's streets (Plate 3.4).

3.1.8 Dredging, weed cutting, clearing and snagging

These activities are commonly grouped together under the umbrella term of *maintenance*. All the methods aim to improve the efficiency of water flow through the river channel by removing obstructions, since reducing channel roughness increases the river flow velocity, and this lowers the flood height and reduces the risk of flooding.

At its simplest, *dredging* requires material to be broken up, loosened and left for the natural river currents to transport downstream. Alternatively, sediment may be removed by mechanical diggers, pumped onto the floodplain or discharged into barges before being dumped at selected locations. The frequency of dredging operations varies with the importance of alleviating the flood risk and the rate of sedimentation. The clay streams in East Anglia, for example, experience much silting and require extensive dredging every 5 to 10 years.

Weed cutting is required in many streams to control the annual growth of aquatic plants, particularly in the highly productive lowland chalk streams in both Great Britain and North America. Although plants physically reduce the capacity of the channel, their main impact is to increase the roughness of the channel which slows the flow of water (due to friction) and increases the accumulation of silt. The prolific growth of aquatic vegetation can also impede the drainage of lowland areas. Massive summer weed growth in the channel is often a direct result of previous felling of riverside trees because waterweeds thrive if they are exposed to sunlight all day, and are additionally nourished by quantities of fertiliser pouring off adjacent fields where there is no longer a buffer strip of trees and shrubs along the river margin. In such streams aquatic plants may be rigorously controlled by cutting several times a year, and the amount of weed removed can be enormous. For example, on the River Frome, a chalk stream in Dorset, the estimated amount of weed removed during a single cut is between 1.3 and 2.6 tonnes per hectare.

Aquatic vegetation (Plate 3.5), including submerged, emergent and marginal plants, can be controlled by herbicides or grazing fish, such as carp, as well as by mechanical cutting.

Plate 3.5   Aquatic vegetation on the River Whitewater, Hampshire, UK.

Clearing and snagging is the removal of fallen trees and debris jams from the channel as well as the harvesting of timber from channel banks and floodplains. As a means of flood control on small streams in North America, the conventional practice has been to remove all obstructions from the channel (snagging) and to take out all significant vegetation within a speci-fied width on both sides of the channel (clearing).

In Britain much tree clearance was undertaken in the 1930s. Tree branches trailing in the water created flood problems whilst whole trees blocked river channels, collecting further material and causing localised scouring of the river bed. Although debris dams on the Highland Water in the New Forest (Plate 3.6) pose a problem for the Forestry Commission by trapping sediment and causing increased overbank flooding at some sites, they are beneficial in reducing the floodpeaks in downstream sections.

Early channel clearance work in New Zealand involved the complete removal of willows by mechanical methods such as traction engines and bulldozers, and follow-up work was often undertaken to spray young growth and stumps. The folly of complete clearance, however, has since

Plate 3.6   Debris dams, Highland Water, New Forest, Hampshire, UK.

come to light, because willows actually form excellent bank protection.

3.1.9   Land drainage

The purpose of land drainage is to lower the water level on land adjacent to the river. Arterial drains increase the efficiency with which surface water, normally from rainfall, is collected and carried to the main watercourses from adjoining fields. Channelisation of the main river, primarily through straightening and deepening, also lowers the water level in the river and further improves the

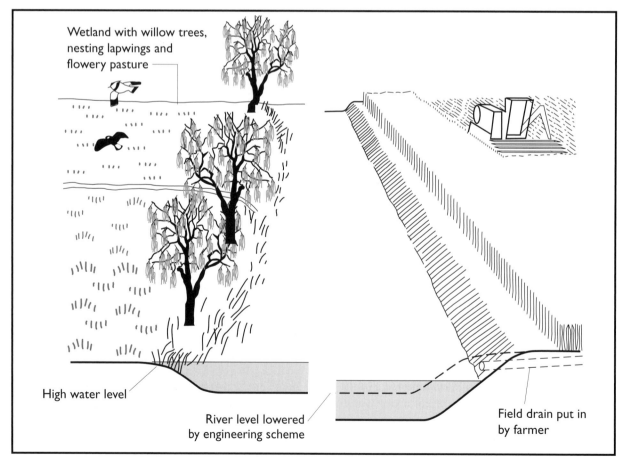

Figure 3.4   The principles of land drainage Source: Purseglove, 1989, p. 213.

evacuation of excess water from the land (Figure 3.4). Pumping operations may also be required to prevent waterlogging.

There has been considerable land drainage in many developed countries to facilitate the intensification of agricultural production, usually from summer grazing to cereal production. Continued drainage then becomes a necessity, because the risk of flooding is a serious problem for cereals since root crops can be completely destroyed if they are submerged for more than 24 hours. Roots of wheat which have been stunted by excessive water in spring will be less able to withstand a summer drought and actual flooding can be disastrous.

In Britain, agricultural drainage schemes have been carried out by a number of organisations during the past 550 years and it was easy to justify drainage operations during periods of food shortage, particularly during the Second World War and in the immediate post-war period when it was vital to maximise agricultural production. However, with the current situation of agricultural food surpluses, the economic and environmental costs of land drainage, arising not only through the engineering operations but from problems such as land deterioration caused by drainage (Purseglove, 1989), the logic of further schemes is being questioned.

3.1.10 Adjusting to the flood hazard

Channelisation has traditionally been the main method of flood management but it can never offer a complete solution to the problem of flooding. Nor is it possible to exert total control on human behaviour in flood-prone areas to offset the flood hazard, because of the numerous and often conflicting political, social and economic pressures to develop floodplains. Individual householders or businesses may, for example, choose to bear the occasional loss because the benefits of a riverside location are so huge. It is, therefore, important to adopt other measures for reducing the impacts of flooding.

Emergency action is an effective adjustment in areas where the frequency of flooding is high. It usually encompasses the evacuation of people and their possessions from the flood hazard area following a flood warning, and the protection of immovable property. The success depends largely on the amount and reliability of the advance warning and on the type of evacuation required, but attempts to raise the alertness of 'at risk'

communities must guard against the 'cry wolf syndrome' which may cause complacency. Although costs from flooding can be high, this approach may still represent one of the most economical adjustments to floods in some river environments.

Flood proofing can be used to reduce the vulnerability of buildings to flooding. These measures range from temporary sandbagging of doorways to permanent, long-term building design features such as installing valves in drains and sewers to prevent floodwaters backing-up, waterproofing of underground telephone cables, anchorage devices to prevent buildings being washed away, and raising houses above the most frequent flood levels.

Land-use regulation promotes the beneficial use of floodplains with a minimum of flood damage and a minimum expenditure on flood protection. Some of the most frequently adopted methods of land-use regulation, particularly in Britain and the USA, are compulsory purchase of land for public uses that are flood tolerant to stop the further intensification of land use; encroachment limits beyond which further expansion is prevented to allow the unimpeded passage of a design flood; and land-use zoning whereby more severe restrictions are placed on land use with increasing proximity to the river.

Financial measures may also be used to modify human responses to the threat of flooding. Schemes of flood insurance, with premiums adjusted to the degree of risk, may not reduce the occupancy of flood-prone areas, but at least only those who can afford the premiums will remain.

Catchment management or source control includes modifying the land use upstream of the flood-risk area to reduce the severity of flood discharges. In this approach the action is taken at the point where the flood is generated rather than waiting to take action downstream at locations where that flood would represent a potential threat. It is based on the 'prevention is better than cure' principle, and useful measures include afforestation and the construction of flood storage areas. These methods are likely to be most effective for small floods in smaller catchments, by reducing flood volumes and delaying flood response. In a large catchment, where floodwaters spend more time travelling in the streams and main river than over the land surface, catchment management is much less effective in reducing the flood problem.

3.2 Managing river channel changes

Bank protection methods and *river training works* are techniques for restraining river channel adjustment mainly by reducing bank erosion. Channel stabilisation is often necessary to protect settlements and agricultural land adjacent to the river and to maintain navigation on larger rivers. Bank slumping through erosion can also impede the river flow and increase the risk of flooding. The practice of dredging, to remove excessive sediment build-up, is a further method for managing river channel adjustment, but it will not be discussed further here as it has already been examined as an important flood control measure.

3.2.1 Bank protection methods

River banks have traditionally been protected by *riprap* (quarried stone), *gabions* (rock-filled wire mattresses) and *revetments* (coverings of resistant materials such as concrete, steel or plastic sheeting). Although riprap (Plate 3.7) is generally the preferred option, gabions have been used extensively on rivers in Italy, Germany and Austria and have been applied in the USA for over 60 years (Plate 3.8). Modern versions consist of a rectangular compartment made from thick steel wire which can be galvanised or coated with plastic. A major advantage of gabions is that the wire mesh allows the rock-filled basket to change shape without failure due to unstable ground or scouring of the river bank by flowing water.

A wide variety of bank protection methods have been used in New Zealand (as summarised in Table 3.2), often following the clearance of bankside vegetation. Stabilisation has also been required where excessive shoaling in braided rivers has caused bank erosion, where flood banks have been threatened by migrating rivers and where bank

Plate 3.8   Gabion mattresses, River Thames, UK.

erosion has been caused by the wash from power boats. Bank protection methods are also commonly applied following resectioning work to support the newly constructed steeper channel banks.

3.2.2 River training works

The most common river training works are *groynes* (also known as *deflectors* or *dikes*) which are structures built to extend from the channel banks into the river, transverse to the river flow. The characteristics of groynes, in particular their spacing, alignment in relation to the flow current, and whether they are impermeable or permeable, varies with the purpose for which the training works are being used. River training can provide bank protection either by deflecting erosive river flows away from vulnerable areas along the channel banks, or by promoting sediment trapping and deposition in areas that have suffered erosion. For example, while a series of permeable groynes will allow water to pass through the struc-tures but induce the deposition of small suspended material between the groynes (Plate 3.9), imper-meable groynes will deflect river flow but promote the trapping of larger bed material (Plate 3.10).

Plate 3.7   Quarry stone riprap.

Plate 3.9   Permeable deflectors on the River White-water, Hampshire, promoting sediment trapping and aquatic plant growth.

Table 3.2   **The wide variety of bank protection methods used in New Zealand**

Procedure	Description
Stake planting	Planting of willow or poplar.
Shingle and stake	Material bulldozed from the bed against low eroding banks and light willow poles or brush placed against the material.
Mattress work	Bank graded and covered with willow or poplar fascines, or loose brush anchored with live stakes or netted stone 'bolsters' can be used to weigh down the fascines. Long line willow or poplar poles can be laid along the bank instead of fascines ('Hayman method').
Pile and fascine revetment	Timber or old rail piles are driven in front of an eroding bank; fascines, brush or branches of willow are then placed between the piles and the bank.
Live pile and stake fence	As above but live poles planted behind the line of piles and held in position with wires; space behind the piles may be filled with material dredged from the channel.
Anchored willow	Large willow or poplar branches are anchored along an eroding river bank and may be planted in a trench with brush end facing downstream and held in place with a wire. Heavier construction to cope with severe bank erosion (e.g. heavy-duty wire weighted with stones).
Rock raking	Using coarse material from bed to place along channel banks.
Netted stone gabions and mattress	Stone-filled gabions.
Spur groynes	Series of short boulder gabion groynes, built normal to the bank or pointing slightly upstream.
Riprap	Placement of quarried stone; size of material depends on local conditions.
Concrete block; concrete or stone; masonry	Used in urban areas at bridge sites.
Sheet pile	Timber or steel, backed with rubble, boulders or concrete.
Heavy pile, cable and netting	Heavy construction used in mountain environments: cables attached to two rows of rails in chevron pattern; netting then attached by wire.
Hedgehogs or sputnics	Concrete blocks with rails set into them.
Concrete tetrahedrons	Heavy blocks that do not roll easily placed in clusters.

Source: Brookes, 1988, p. 34 (after Acheson, 1968).

Alternatively, river training structures can be used to deflect erosive river flows onto channel deposits that pose problems for navigation or flood control, to promote their removal through scouring. Groynes have been used extensively on the Mississippi River in this way to maintain a navigation channel without recourse to expensive dredging. By constricting the flow area, velocities are locally increased, shoals are scoured and secondary channels and chutes are closed, so that all flow is confined to the main channel which then deepens.

3.3   Conclusions

Channelisation, however sophisticated and extensive, cannot guarantee complete protection against flooding and its associated channel form adjustments. This is because it is physically impossible to control the very rare high-magnitude flood events except by designing all flood defences against a correctly estimated maximum possible flood. Furthermore, some river engineering schemes have resulted in changes in the river environment that were not anticipated at the design

Plate 3.10   Impermeable deflector.

and implementation stages, such as sedimentation problems, and these can necessitate costly maintenance activities to keep the structures operating at their design specification.

There are also fears that river engineering practices may have worsened flooding on some rivers. One such dispute concerns the impacts of river engineering on the Mississippi. Critics argue that while levees work well for small annual floods which are easily contained, larger floods such as the 1993 flood are made more dangerous because constricting the river forces the water upwards instead of allowing it to spread out across the floodplain. The water then backs up, causing unnecessary flooding elsewhere, and the added pressure means that when a levee breaks, the flood is much more violent than it would be during a natural river rise.

The Corps of Engineers are adamant, however, that channelisation cannot be blamed for the recent rises in flood levels on the Mississippi. Although the levees do make water somewhat higher inside the levees, the flood control reservoirs along the river counterbalance this. They also repel criticism about the performance of the levees in the 1993 flood. The flood was created by exceptional rainfall and the levees were not designed and built for the resulting flood elevation. The elevation for flood protection was chosen because of economics, but that does not mean that the levees failed. And so the arguments continue.

The disputes over engineering of the Mississippi River may never be fully resolved, but there are many studies throughout the world that have documented a wide range of physical, chemical and biological impacts arising from conventional river engineering practices. These impacts are examined in Chapter 4.

Points to consider and things to do

- Make a list of major floodplain settlements in the world.

- Find out if there are any 'lost' rivers in your nearest town or city.

- Summarise the aims of conventional river engineering.

- For your home region, or for places you have visited, try to identify the engineering practices described in this chapter. Find as many examples as possible. In each case try to find out why the scheme was undertaken.

- Many channelisation projects have been designed for the 100-year flood event. What are the problems with this?

- Present the arguments for and against river channelisation.

4   Consequences of traditional river engineering

- *How has channelisation affected the physical, chemical and biological nature of rivers and their floodplains?*

- *What are the implications of these impacts for the way river environments are managed?*

In 1974 a book entitled *The River Killers* was published. The author, Martin Heuvelmans, called for the abolition of the US Corps of Engineers and voiced some very strong public criticism in the USA over channelisation and its impacts. At the same time, practical handbooks on how to oppose river engineering projects started to appear, and US citizens turned to the courts to obtain injunctions.

One such court battle, over the planned excavation of Chicod Creek in North Carolina, turned out to be a landmark case (Brookes, 1988, pp. 54–55). The channelisation project was successfully opposed on the grounds that a satisfactory Environmental Impact Statement had not been

produced and the inquiry forced changes both in the construction techniques, to minimise environmental impact, and in the planning philosophy of river channelisation.

A similarly historic case was fought in the UK in 1978 over the proposed draining of Amberley Wild Brooks, forming part of the River Arun floodplain in West Sussex. This case represented the first public enquiry into a drainage scheme in England and Wales. The Inspector criticised the insufficient consultation on the part of the Water Authority, who had proposed the drainage operation, and recommended that the scheme should not go ahead because of the unique conservation interest of the

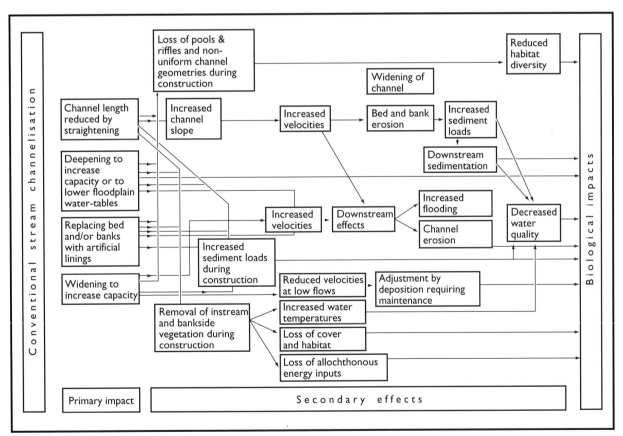

Figure 4.1   Impacts of channelisation   Source: Brookes, 1988, p. 23.

Note: Primary impacts are changes caused by the engineering procedures and are restricted to the modified sections. Secondary impacts are the result of these channelisation procedures and mostly occur in the downstream reaches, although some impacts can be transmitted upstream along tributaries. The physical changes all have knock-on effects on the stream biology.

site (18 hectares of the wetland had previously been designated a Site of Special Scientific Interest).

This concern over the wide range of physical, chemical and biological impacts of river channelisation (Figure 4.1) has triggered many studies attempting to establish the full effects of particular engineering procedures in a range of river environments. Such knowledge is vital as the basis for implementing alternative, environmentally-sensitive designs.

4.1 Geomorphological, hydrological and water quality impacts

River engineering deliberately changes the river environment for the purposes of flood and erosion control but it can also result in many further and often unexpected morphological, hydrological and water quality impacts (Brookes, 1988). These impacts are not simply confined to the channelised river section but may be transmitted to the downstream and upstream reaches and along tributary streams. A further complication is that channelisation often involves a combination of measures and the individual effects of each operation are therefore difficult to isolate.

4.1.1 Impacts on river channel morphology

Channel straightening increases channel slope and flow velocities and, as a result, sediment transport also increases. If this sediment transport rate exceeds the supply of sediment, degradation of the river bed occurs, often progressing in an upstream direction. Erosion of the river bed may also lead to the collapse of river banks. In the unmodified downstream reach, the deposition of excess sediment is a common response. This then increases the risk of overbank flooding, and dredging may become necessary to maintain the

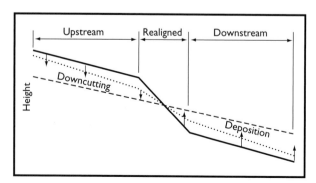

Figure 4.2   Degradation in straightened alluvial channels Source: Parker & Andres, 1976.

channel capacity. By the processes of upstream degradation and downstream aggradation, the river channel gradient is gradually lowered to its original slope (Figure 4.2). In the New Forest, England, a number of realigned and enlarged streams achieved stability in under ten years largely through the process of bed degradation (Tuckfield, 1980). But other river systems may remain unstable for much longer.

Rivers that have been straightened without subsequent bank protection also have a tendency to regain their former sinuosity; this recovery process has been observed on a reach of the River Ystwyth, a gravel-bed river in Wales (Lewin, 1976) and on straightened rivers in Denmark (Figure 4.3).

The nature and extent of adjustments that take place after channel straightening depend on the erodibility of the bed and bank sediments (Brice, 1981) and the stream's available energy for erosion, known as its stream power. In Denmark, Brookes (1987c) observed how the most powerful stream sites (with stream power values greater than 35 Watts per square metre) underwent erosion following realignment, whereas the low-energy stream sites changed very little.

All the above examples demonstrate why realignment often necessitates long-term maintenance operations. River adjustments can also have serious implications for structures built adjacent to, or across their channels. For example, bridges may have to be reinforced, lengthened or even replaced if river channels begin to enlarge through erosion.

Widening a channel increases the river's ability to contain flood flows, but at low discharges the flow velocities are reduced because of the larger area of contact between the water and the channel boundary. The river thus becomes less able to transport sediment at the more frequent, lower, flows and the deposited sediments may in time become stabilised to form permanent bar features and channel islands to give a braided flow pattern. In the River Tame, England, for example, deposition of a berm returned the enlarged channel to its original size in less than 30 years following engineering in 1930.

Enlarging a channel by *deepening* can cause the river bed to degrade both downstream and upstream from the point of dredging. Deepening the main river also lowers the base-levels of tributary streams which may in turn suffer rapid

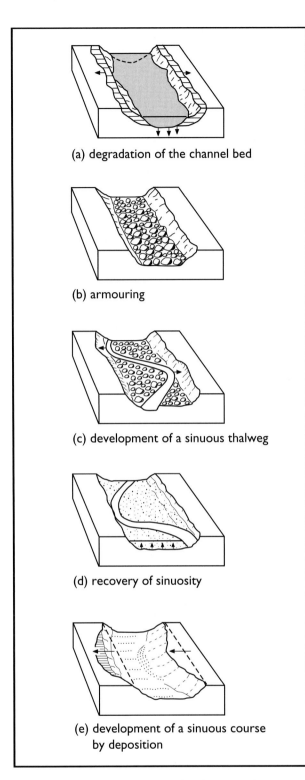

(a) degradation of the channel bed

(b) armouring

(c) development of a sinuous thalweg

(d) recovery of sinuosity

(e) development of a sinuous course
by deposition

Figure 4.3   Principal types of adjustment in straightened river channels in Denmark   Source: Brookes, 1987c.

upstream erosion. Further complications can then arise when sediment eroded from the tributaries is deposited in the main channel. Over time, however, a balance between sediment load and sediment transport capacity will be restored. The nature and degree of channel adjustments following resectioning is also related to stream power. Streams in high-energy environments (upland

streams) are likely to erode following resectioning and eventually recover their original dimensions whereas streams in low-energy environments (lowland streams) do not seem to react.

Various river adjustments have been recorded following *bank protection works*. Along channels lined with concrete it is often necessary to remove sediment which tends to accumulate above the artificial channel boundary, whereas along channels protected by riprap or gabions, morphological adjustments are common if the channel has been deepened, widened and straightened prior to protection. The most dramatic changes tend to take place during flood events and the structures may even be destroyed. Quarry-stone riprap and gabions were used to protect a resectioned reach of the Afon Trannon, a gravel-bed river in Wales, but the structures failed and the channel reformed a meandering pattern at low to medium flows. The failure seems to have arisen because the river's bed sediments were used to protect the banks, there were inadequate foundations to avoid basal scouring of the riprap and gabions, and the structures were placed too close to strong erosive secondary flow currents (Newson, 1986).

Morphological adjustments may arise after *embanking* a channel because the heightened banks contain larger flows with greater velocities. One outcome is degradation of the river bed, and possibly the banks as well, which may necessitate associated bank protection schemes. Another is the accusation that levees raise flood heights and cause increased flooding in unprotected reaches.

Diversion channels which flow back into the main river may cause either deposition or erosion at the point where they re-enter. If the bedload is unchanged but the stream discharge is reduced by the diversion, deposition may occur in the form of depositional bars or sediment in-filling in pools. As deposits accumulate the channel capacity will be steadily reduced, increasing the risk of flooding in the river reaches downstream of the diversion channel. Conversely, if the bedload is reduced but the discharge is not, the bed and banks of the channel may erode resulting in an increase in channel cross-sectional area. This erosion will continue downstream until channel stability is attained. In Alkali Creek in Wyoming, flow returning from a diversion channel caused the channel to degrade to a layer of large gravel and cobbles and the river banks required protection measures to prevent erosion (Vanoni, 1975).

38

The purpose of *river training structures* is to induce changes in the river environment, but the specific impacts of different dike and groyne designs, particularly the impact of their location on sediment movement and flow hydrology, are still insufficiently understood. The structures may change the local slope of an alluvial river and redistribute the flow velocities, causing either local scour or sedimentation.

Finally, *weed cutting* and *clearing and snagging* operations increase the hydraulic efficiency of the channel but also increase the flow velocities adjacent to the channel bank and reduce the bank's resistance to erosion. As a consequence, the removal of debris and bankside vegetation often causes bank erosion and channel widening.

4.1.2 Hydrology

Numerous observations suggest that straightening and shortening channels and removing obstructions to the flow of water results in a faster delivery of water to downstream river reaches. This reduces the flood risk in the engineered section but increases the likelihood of downstream flooding. However, there have been relatively few quantitative studies of the hydrological impacts of channelisation. One exception is the study by Campbell *et al.* (1972) of the effect of channel straightening on the movement of a single flood wave along the Boyer River in western Iowa.

These researchers observed that at all 36 study cross-sections the peak discharge increased, the time base of the discharge hydrograph shortened and the time of travel of the flood wave downstream was reduced (Figure 4.4). The consequence for downstream floodplain dwellers is a larger flood wave with reduced flood warning times. A more recent study on the Raba River, Poland (Wyzga, 1996) has also shown how channelisation has shifted the flood hazard downstream. A reduction of flood storage has increased flood discharge on this river by nearly 2.5 times.

Land drainage works also increase flood discharges. For example, arterial drainage works completed between 1955 and 1972 increased the size of the 3-year flood by between 3 and 118 per cent for 12 catchments in Ireland (Bree and Cunnane, 1980) due to the elimination of floodplain storage and the improved hydraulic efficiency of the channels. The dramatic impact of reducing flood storage is also illustrated by the Massachusetts Water Resources Commission's (1971) estimate that a reduction of only 10 per cent of the wetland storage of the Neponset River basin would cause a 46 cm increase in the flood height.

Research is currently being undertaken at the Institute of Hydrology at Wallingford, England, to investigate the hydrological impacts of a range of channel works throughout the UK.

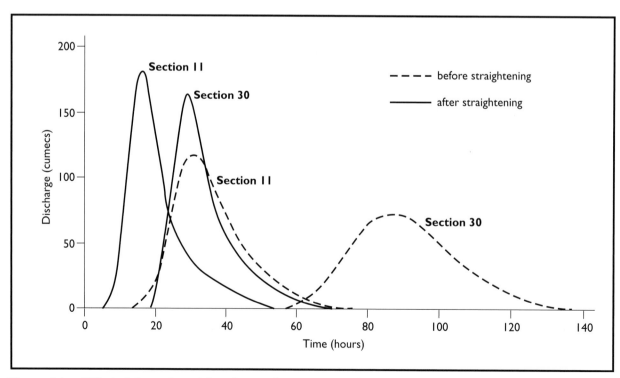

Figure 4.4 Effect of channel straightening on the movement of a single flood wave
Source: Campbell *et al.*, 1972.

4.1.3 Water quality

Channelisation can affect a large number of water quality variables including total suspended sediment, streamflow velocity, temperature, turbidity, colour, conductance, pH, dissolved oxygen and concentration of faecal coliforms. Water quality impacts will be site-specific, reflecting catchment characteristics, the severity of the channel modification and the length of the recovery period after engineering.

Increased sediment loads downstream from channelisation works reach a peak during dredging and immediately after construction when erosion of unvegetated banks is at a maximum. On the River Wylye, near Salisbury, Wiltshire, 514 tonnes (312 m^3) of sediment were released to downstream reaches of the river as a result of realignment works over a period of 15 working days (Brookes, 1983) and sediment levels were 40 times greater than normal.

Conventional river engineering results in the removal of trees, undercut banks, rocks and debris, which all provide shade in natural river channels. Channelisation thus increases both the mean daily temperature and the range of daily temperatures. Realignment of the Yellow Creek in north-east Mississippi over a distance of 9.6 km caused the average daily maximum stream temperature to increase by 4°C. In assessing the overall impact, however, the critical issue is whether water temperature changes exceed the tolerance of aquatic fauna and flora.

The impacts of channelisation on water chemistry are wide-ranging. During dredging on the Yellow Creek, north-east Mississippi, the water quality changes reflected the increased sediment input and the changed nature of the sediments. Mean values of specific conductance, turbidity, colour, chemical oxygen demand, total alkalinity, hardness, ammonia, phosphorus, sulphate, iron, lead and manganese were observed to be between 50 and 100 per cent greater than normal (Shields and Sanders, 1986). Estimated average daily loadings of total metal, nutrients and dissolved solids and concentrations of faecal coliforms were also greater during construction because dredging causes disturbance and relocation of river-bed sediments. Following engineering, water quality also tends to show much greater temporal variability within channelised reaches, mainly due to the increased flow velocities and the impact of channel maintenance activities.

4.2   Impacts on river ecology

Channelisation not only directly removes river fauna and flora during engineering but also causes physical disturbance to the river environment which has longer-term consequences for river ecology. The main effect of channelisation is to reduce the habitat diversity and the number of ecological niches. The quality and functions of the species occupying the river system may also change as they try to adapt to the new conditions. Figure 4.5 provides a visual comparison of the channel morphology and hydrology of a natural stream with a channelised watercourse. The diagram shows the various habitats that are typically altered or destroyed during construction and the associated impact on river flora and fauna.

It is now known which engineering operations are most harmful to river ecology (Table 4.1). The impacts on invertebrates, fish and aquatic plants arise mainly from channel excavation and dredging, the lining of channels, clearing and snagging and weed cutting. The habitats of birds and mammals may also be destroyed by the

Table 4.1   **Types of channel modification listed in ascending order of impact on fish and wildlife resources**

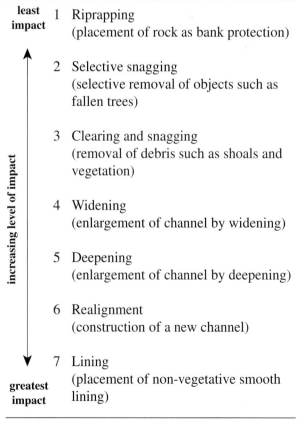

least impact	1	Riprapping (placement of rock as bank protection)
	2	Selective snagging (selective removal of objects such as fallen trees)
	3	Clearing and snagging (removal of debris such as shoals and vegetation)
increasing level of impact	4	Widening (enlargement of channel by widening)
	5	Deepening (enlargement of channel by deepening)
	6	Realignment (construction of a new channel)
greatest impact	7	Lining (placement of non-vegetative smooth lining)

Source: Soil Conservation Service, 1977.

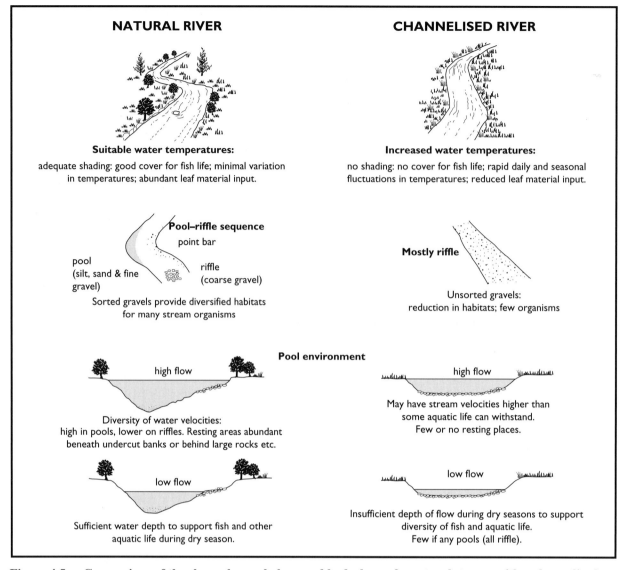

Figure 4.5   Comparison of the channel morphology and hydrology of a natural stream with a channelised watercourse   Source: Corning, 1975 (and in Brookes, 1988, p. 112).

removal of bankside trees, bushes and plants during construction. However, channelisation works that are intended to facilitate drainage for agriculture may have far-reaching effects which extend onto the floodplain (see section 4.3) and the draining of wetlands can thus have very serious consequences for mammals, amphibians, insects, birds and plants throughout the whole river environment.

4.2.1 Effects on flora

River flora include submerged plants growing within the channel, emergent species growing at the margins of the channel, riparian vegetation growing on the river banks, and plants growing on the floodplain or in adjacent wetland areas. These plants play a vital role in providing shelter and protection to macro-invertebrates and fish, by shading watercourses from excessive temperatures,

providing an input of organic leaf litter, producing oxygen and by protecting river banks and river beds against erosion. Plants also diversify local conditions, for example by altering flow velocities and the detailed pattern of silt deposition.

Plant types vary within the river environment according to physical (flow velocity, substrate), chemical (nutrients in the silt), or biotic (shading by larger plants or grazing by animals) differences. River engineering affects flora through physical destruction of the habitat or by modifying the factors that control plant growth and survival.

Resectioning smooths a river's bed and banks and this reduces plant diversity. If the bed is unbroken by dredging then plants recover quickly, but if the bed is destroyed and the underground parts of the plant are removed during dredging, recovery may not occur for 5 to 10 years. Generally, species return to a site within two years of dredging in British rivers, and the amount of vegetation is back to normal after three years (Haslam, 1978). Alternatively, new species may begin to invade and colonise if the river conditions change, for example *Ranunculus* will invade a gravel river bed exposed by dredging.

Brookes (1987a) has assessed the recovery of a number of streams in southern England following river engineering works. On the Wallop Brook in Hampshire, England (Figure 4.6), regrowth occurred from plant rhizomes remaining in the channel bed after shallow excavation in December 1981 and recovery was relatively rapid, but in most cases regeneration appeared to depend on the invasion of plant propagules moving from upstream. During the second growing season the standing crop of the excavated channel generally attained the value recorded in the control reach. The successful recovery on the Wallop Brook was possible because valley gravels extended for several metres below the bed of this chalk stream and therefore the substrate available for colonisation by plants was not substantially changed by excavation. By comparison, relatively little recovery of vegetation occurred in two years after excavation of the Ober Water, a clay-bed stream in the New Forest, where the original substrate was destroyed and replaced by bedrock.

The new width and depth dimensions of an excavated channel are also important in determining the degree of ecological impact. Deepened channel sections may preclude the development of plants by reducing or eliminating the light available for plant growth at the river bed. In over-deepened pools the accumulation of silt deposits (because of the reduced flow velocities) may permanently blanket the substrate, thereby encouraging the growth of silt-loving plant varieties. On the other hand, a widened section may support a greater total standing crop because of the increased area of bed suitable for colonisation, although over-widening does reduce the column of water in which plants can grow.

By releasing sediment, dredging can also affect river vegetation in the downstream reaches: suspended material may abrade the shoots of plants and prevent photosynthesis by smothering leaves; silt may be deposited above gravel causing plants to root in unstable conditions (and be washed away by the next flood!) or it may lead to the burial of aquatic plant communities; and when the organic content is high, silt can create anaerobic conditions around the roots, although it usually improves the nutrient status.

A study of the impact of suspended sediment was undertaken on the Wallop Brook in Hampshire

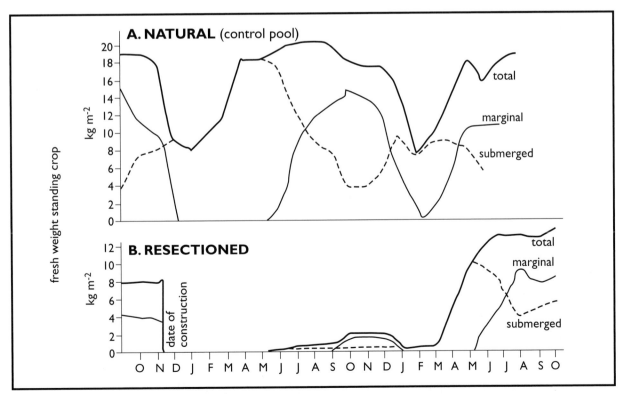

Figure 4.6   **Recovery of the standing crop of aquatic vegetation in resectioned reaches of the Wallop Brook, Hampshire, England, during 1981 and 1982** Source: Brookes, 1987a.

following channelisation in 1981 (Brookes, 1986). A comparison was made between the downstream reaches affected by sedimentation and upstream control reaches. The aquatic plant species were affected differently by sedimentation – *Ranunculus* was unable to vary its rooting level in response to the sedimentation and was therefore smothered, whilst *Nasturtium* was able to adjust its rooting depth and it thrived.

Weed cutting not only reduces the plant cover in the river but also disrupts the growth patterns of a number of species. For example, weed cutting by hand on the Candover Brook in November 1972 – a chalk stream in Hampshire, England – reduced the plant cover from 48 per cent to 8 per cent and the mean dry weight standing biomass from 168 gm^{-2} to 32 gm^{-2}. Although *Callitriche* remained the most dominant plant, it covered only 50 per cent of the area prior to the cut; it could not outgrow other plants as it would do normally following overwintering, partly because substantial amounts of silt had been washed out after the cut. Further complications can arise because plants have distinctive growth patterns, and there is a particular time of year when cutting is more effective in controlling one plant rather than another. For example, if *Ranunculus* is cut during its growing season in the spring, this stimulates further growth rather than reducing it.

4.2.2 Effects on fauna

Invertebrates. Many different factors determining the occurrence and detailed distribution of invertebrates can be changed by channelisation (Table 4.2). These include river flow velocity, water temperature, the river sediments, vegetation, and dissolved substances. Other important factors are liability to floods and drought, food supply, competition between species, and shade.

River flow velocity – both its mean value and its variability over time and space – controls the occurrence and abundance of invertebrate species and therefore the whole structure of the animal community. Many invertebrates rely on the water current either for feeding or respiration, and ecologists have found that particular species are confined to fairly definite ranges of flow velocity. Where the velocities are persistently high at a site then almost all species may be absent. Conversely, slow flow or stagnant watercourses, which accumulate a large amount of silt, can only be tolerated by a limited number of species. Some invertebrates such as *Simulium* larvae move to sheltered positions (known as flow refugia) when river discharge increases, whilst others (e.g. mayfly nymphs) are adapted to live in crevices beneath and between stones, and some only colonise the

Table 4.2 **Examples of the impacts of channelisation on macro-invertebrates**

Location	Type	Variables affected	Altered parameters
Rush Creek, California (USA)	Realigned	Changed substrate; lack of pools and shade.	Biomass of invertebrates per unit area reduced by 75%.
Buena Vista Marsh, Portage Co, Wisconsin (USA)	Dredging	Seasonal effect; substrate only unstable at high flow; at other times vegetation.	High invertebrate populations when substrate stable; vegetation and silt favours snails/midges. Elimination of stoneflies.
Mill-stream Dorset, England	Dredging	Substrate disrupted.	Population density of benthos reduced to 4,000 individuals/m^2 but increased by 80–86% in 2 years.
River Hull, Yorkshire, England	Resectioning	Substrate disrupted but largely unchanged.	Benthos escaped the bucket and redistributed rapidly over the affected substrate.
Gjern Stream Jutland, Denmark	Annual cutting of macrophytes	Habitat destroyed by removing macrophytes.	99% increase of total drift density.

Source: information from Brookes, 1983.

protected downstream faces of cobbles and boulders.

Channelisation affects water temperatures and oxygen levels (because the solubility of oxygen decreases steadily with rising water temperature). In unpolluted freshwater rivers, oxygen concentrations rarely fall below critical levels, but in river backwaters oxygen may reach very low concentrations during the summer. The respiratory rate of certain invertebrates is related to water temperature, and a number of research studies have reported a correlation between shade and the occurrence or abundance of particular species such as mayflies.

Dredging has the most severe impact on river fauna because animals such as freshwater mussels may be physically removed and other macro-invertebrates may fail to re-establish because of a changed channel substrate. Silt deposits are especially problematic because they screen out light and tend to hold extraneous substances, such as industrial wastes, on the stream bed. Sand or shifting silt on the bed may also eliminate shelter, which can have a long-term effect. The replacement of pebbles by fine sand in the engineered reaches of the Luxapalila River seems to have been responsible for their lower standing crop, productivity, species diversity and number of macro-invertebrates compared with undisturbed reaches, for in excess of 52 years after channelisation (Arner et al., 1975; 1976).

Clearing and snagging operations cause deposits of leaves, twigs and fine-grained sediments (which are frequently an important habitat for many invertebrates) to be washed downstream. However, the impact of annual weed cutting can be even more damaging, and it is probable that in streams that undergo annual cutting, susceptible species may already have disappeared. Weed cutting on the Gjern stream in Jutland, Denmark, for example, increased the drifting of fauna downstream. The total drift density increased by 173 times, to a maximum of 24,722 invertebrates per 100 m^3, and even several days after cutting the drift density of many species was significantly higher than before cutting (Kern-Hansen, 1978).

Fish. The impact of channelisation on invertebrates is enormous, but much of the ecological concern over traditional river engineering has centred upon the effects on fish. Morphological, and therefore habitat, diversity within stream channels is essential for the movement, breeding, feeding and shelter of fish, but traditional engineering practices create homogeneous rivers. The principal abiotic factors that affect fish populations are temperature (both directly and indirectly through the influence of oxygen consumption), rate of flow and discharge fluctuations, and the availability of suitable shelter. All of these factors can be altered by channelisation (Table 4.3). For example, straightening a river reduces the available habitat (including areas for resting and sheltering) by creating a more uniform environment. This reduces the total number of fish and the number of fish species and also poses problems for migrating fish (Keller, 1976).

The impacts of river engineering on fish (Table 4.4) are evident almost immediately after construction. Whilst the initial cause of fish populations moving out of a channelised reach may be a behavioural response (Swales, 1982a), the severity and longevity of this impact is determined by the exact nature of the habitat changes. Channelisation may affect several of the habitat features listed in Table 4.3; therefore it is difficult to isolate individual causes for the changes in fish populations. Studies suggest that changes in the physical rather than the chemical form of the habitat are mainly responsible, since pH values, dissolved minerals and gases may undergo little alteration; whereas changes to sediment loads, temperature and physical habitat elements, such as the removal of riffles and pools, seem to be the most damaging to fish populations.

Salmonids (e.g. Atlantic salmon, brown trout, sea trout) require definite nest-sites in gravel substances, known as 'redds', and are therefore particularly susceptible to dredging operations or engineering works that disturb the natural channel substrate. Many coarse fish, including barbel, chub and dace, also spawn on gravel or aquatic or marginal vegetation and use weed beds as nurseries for fry and juveniles. Sediment released during dredging may therefore have a considerable impact. Although adult fish can generally tolerate substantial amounts of suspended sediment, silt deposits can blanket portions of the stream bottom, eliminating potential spawning grounds and reducing the available food by killing bottom-dwelling organisms.

Fish populations also suffer in channelised reaches through the removal of bankside and in-stream vegetation. First, trout populations, in particular

44

Table 4.3   **Major habitat requirements of fish**

A. *Movement and breeding*
- Migrations and other movements either up- or down-stream require an absence of serious obstacles and adequate water depth and velocity.
- Fish require a suitable substrate for spawning; requirements vary with individual species. Many species require a gravel or stony substrate (e.g. salmonids). Other species require rock surfaces or aquatic plants.
- Incubation of eggs requires a stable substrate, adequate water movement, oxygen supply and temperature.

B. *Feeding habits*
- Availability of suitable food (e.g. invertebrates which require suitable bed material or plant species).

C. *Shelter and cover*
- At high flows shelter is required from abnormally high water velocities; cover is needed for protection against predators. At all flows fish require suitable resting places. These conditions are provided by pools, overhanging banks, boulders, in-stream and bank vegetation, tree roots and debris.

Source: Brookes, 1988, p. 126.

Table 4.4   **Examples of the impacts of channelisation on fish**

Location	Type	Date	Variables affected	Reduced parameters	(%)	Recovery
Chariton River, Missouri, USA	Resectioned	1940s	Loss of habitat/ cover for fish	No. of species Total standing crop Standing crop	38 87 98	Values given are for 30 years after construction
Olentangy River, Ohio, USA	Widened, deepened and straightened	1950	Shallow, silty banks unstable	Total number of species	22	Studied 24–25 years after channelisation
Rush Creek, Modoc Co., California, USA	Realigned	1969	Destruction of pool/riffle sequence reduced invertebrates	Trout biomass Total number Total biomass	86 36 49	After 5 years
Flint Creek, Montana, USA	Resectioned	1956	Destruction of habitat	Total biomass	93	After 11 years
North Carolina Coastal Plain streams, USA	Resectioned	no date available	Reduced stream cover; higher temperatures; lack of pools	No. of game fish Species diversity Carrying capacity Weight of game fish	75 28 75 75	After 15 years with no maintenance

Source: information from Brookes, 1983, pp. 123–5.

brown trout, are adversely affected because they require features in the river that provide concealment. Secondly, removal of near-stream deciduous vegetation may result in reduced invertebrate and fish populations as a result of the loss of organic matter to the food chain. And thirdly, loss of overhanging vegetation may create excessive illumination and water temperatures. Cold-water fish such as trout quickly become stressed in channelised river sections because their metabolic rate rises sharply with temperature while oxygen concentrations fall. Furthermore, for trout to breed the water temperature must fall below 14°C at some time of the year.

There have been relatively few studies of the impact of maintenance activities on fish populations although qualitative evidence suggests that weed cutting can have severe effects on river ecology and cause a decline of fisheries over several years (Swales, 1980; 1982b; Mills, 1981). Weed cutting seems to affect fisheries by disrupting fish feeding, reproduction and normal behaviour patterns but it can be difficult to distinguish between natural fluctuations in population levels and those that may arise from weed-cutting activities. What is known is that regular channel maintenance hinders the recovery of fish populations after channelisation. The recovery process also depends on the type and extent of channelisation. Where a channel has been realigned over a considerable distance and replaced by a straight channel, recovery may take up to 1,000 years (Ryckborst, 1980) but if only short lengths of river have been modified, fish may return very quickly from temporary refuge areas (Hansen, 1971).

4.3 Impacts of land drainage

Apart from the desired effect of water-level lowering to improve land for agriculture, drainage has had a number of unfortunate impacts on the river environment. Purseglove (1989) details a large number of these including the loss of floodplain wetlands, the disappearance of wetland fauna and flora and a reduction of species diversity, reduction of soil fertility, soil erosion, increased flood risks, water quality problems, peat wastage, and agricultural over-production.

The disappearance of wetlands has been one cost of agricultural intensification. Even in the last four decades the River Idle washlands in Nottingham-shire and large parts of Romney Marsh, Otmoor, and the Lancashire mosses have been lost; and in the years between 1971 and 1980, an annual average of 207,217 acres (83,858 hectares) was estimated to have been drained in England and Wales, of which 'new' drainage of wetlands comprised around 20,000 acres (8,000 hectares) per year. Major debates have been held since the late 1970s over the future of wetlands in Sussex, Somerset, Yorkshire and East Anglia, and in 1983 the chief scientist of the Nature Conservancy Council produced a report on the destruction of habitat in Great Britain since 1949. Among the casualties wholly or partly attributable to drainage were 97 per cent of the herb-rich haymeadows, 50 per cent of lowland fens and 60 per cent of lowland raised mires, all lost in the space of a generation. In the mid-1980s the Norfolk Broads were losing a staggering 1,500 acres (600 hectares) per year on average.

Land drainage schemes result in wetland fauna and flora being replaced by species that thrive under drier conditions. The fauna lost are those directly dependent on surface water (amphibians, insects and fish in the nursery and breeding pond areas), those dependent on wetland vegetation for cover (beaver, mink, muskrat, otter and salamanders) and those unable to compete with other species which colonise following drainage (deer, pheasants, grouse, partridge). The effects are complex because removal of surface water can substantially reduce or eliminate frog populations and other amphibians, together with insects, and this then reduces the food available to many other types of wildlife. In 1983 the RSPB concluded that land drainage is catastrophic for breeding and wintering wetland birds, arising from changes in the water status of the catchment area and associated changes in land use practices. Wetland drainage in the Kissimmee River Project in Florida had a devastating effect by almost totally eliminating migrating waterfowl (Brookes, 1988, p. 161).

Dryland tree species, such as aspen and poplar, begin to invade drained floodplains and the growth patterns of established trees are affected. Whereas drainage of bog areas in Scandinavia has markedly improved the growth of coniferous forest, in other countries the drainage of hardwood forests may be detrimental, causing the death of older trees and a general reduction in growth rate where the water table is permanently lowered.

With the elimination or reduction of overbank flooding, large quantities of nutrients and valuable fresh water are lost to floodplains. Soil fertility declines and fertilisers are required to sustain intensive agriculture. Declining soil fertility also increases the likelihood of soil erosion problems. Accelerated wind erosion has occurred in the drained wetlands of the East Anglian fens, but also on the fine sands and silts of Lancashire, the Dee estuary, the Nottinghamshire carrs, and the Vale of York. Hedges traditionally provided buffer strips between fields and the riverside, acting as barriers to wind and water erosion, but their removal has increased the amount of topsoil and fertilisers entering streams. And to prevent the silted watercourses from flooding, further dredging may be necessary! Flooding, affecting whole villages, as a result of soil runoff has taken place in Shepton

Beauchamp in Somerset and Ashford-in-the-Water in Derbyshire.

Flooding may also be increased by agricultural land drainage and urbanisation of floodplains because both reduce the storage areas for rainwater and floodwater in a catchment and increase the rates of catchment runoff. As a consequence, river levels rise faster in response to rainfall and flood peaks become greater.

Peat wastage is probably the most visible example of land degradation resulting from wetland drainage. Peat wastes as a result of shrinkage, oxidation and bacterial action, all triggered by the drying effect of drainage upon peat. A 10-year trial by the Ministry of Agriculture, started in 1980 on the Norfolk peat marshes near Acle, measured a fall in ground-level of 2.5 cm each year. The level of peat fenland in Cambridgeshire has fallen by up to 4.6 m since 1650 but 3.9 m since 1850 (Purseglove, 1989, p. 83). Estimates of wastage can also be made by assessing the height at which roads and even some wartime pillboxes stand above the adjacent level of the fens.

As the peat wastes, drainage of the land deteriorates, and so the drainage ditches are deepened leading to further wastage. Once the peat has wasted, poor acid subsoils, especially clays, are often all that remain beneath, and these soils may be insufficiently fertile even for growing potatoes; but such downgraded land will still have to be pumped and embanked to prevent flooding. This situation is further worsened by the projected rise in sea-level due to global warming and the fact that eastern England is steadily falling in relation to the level of the North Sea due to the tilt of the land from isostatic readjustment.

Land drainage, to achieve intensification of agriculture, has thus been an expensive exercise, and over-production of food has now emerged as a further cost of 'taming the flood' (Purseglove, 1989). There is an urgent ecological and economic need, therefore, to redefine farming practice which takes into account the interests of good, long-term husbandry. The development of alternative uses for floodplain wetlands, including their use as natural water storage systems, needs to play a major part in the sustainable management of wetland resources and river environments.

Points to consider and things to do

- Make a comprehensive list of the impacts of river channelisation, indicating which impacts can occur in the channelised reach, downstream of the channelised reach and upstream of the channelised reach.

- Select what you consider to be the 10 most serious impacts of traditional river engineering, and justify your selection. Compare your list with the lists of fellow students. Are there any differences? If so, what are they and why have they arisen?

- Debate the reasons for and against land drainage schemes.

5 Revised approaches to river engineering

- *What lessons have been learnt from the mistakes of traditional river engineering?*

- *Have these lessons been translated into new approaches?*

- *Can river environments be managed in a sympathetic and sustainable way?*

'We may reduce the dredging of rivers, but if we stop it altogether, floods will return to overwhelm us. We are therefore committed to managing rivers, as we are to managing every square mile of the English countryside. It is the way we do so which counts' (Purseglove, 1989, p. 19).

Revised river management techniques aim to alleviate the problems of flooding and river channel adjustment through ways that minimise the environmental impact. Environmentally sensitive or sympathetic river management is possible if the river is treated both as a dynamic geomorphological system and as an ecosystem and not simply as a conduit for water.

The physical and ecological impacts of channelisation can be minimised by:

- selecting the least-damaging options at the design stage based on environmental assessments;

- following recommendations for improved construction and maintenance procedures; and

- using designs that reproduce the characteristics of natural rivers and which, most importantly, preserve the morphological diversity of rivers.

5.1 Selecting the management options

A good way to begin all river management schemes is to undertake a thorough review of existing case studies. This will provide information on the known environmental impacts of different options and will indicate the likely effects of the proposed engineering works. Once an engineering proposal has been put forward, it should be appraised by an interdisciplinary team of experts and discussed with local environmental interest groups. All these responses can then be considered

alongside the environmental impact assessment, now a frequent statutory requirement. Figure 5.1 contrasts the traditional and holistic approaches to river management. The holistic route was developed and first applied by Thames Water in the mid-1980s and involves a four-stage appraisal process: first, the exact nature of the problem is defined; secondly, baseline surveys are conducted to gather all the necessary information; thirdly, a range of options are evaluated, including the 'do nothing' option; and only after these stages is the final option selected. This appraisal process represents a much better approach to decision-making and is the way forward for all new river management schemes.

5.2 Revised construction and maintenance methods

To reduce the damage to river environments caused by channelisation, a number of 'golden rules' should be followed.

- Minimise the length of river that will be disturbed, particularly the amount of channel excavation.

- Employ construction methods and equipment that will minimise damage to river fauna and flora. Educate all construction workers on the need for minimal damage to the stream and encourage them to use their knowledge of local wildlife to avoid damage to sensitive habitats. Use waterborne machinery where possible to ensure minimal removal and damage to trees and other riparian vegetation, and always dredge in an upstream direction so that displaced river fauna can recolonise downstream.

- Preserve as many of the original river sediments as possible or replace large rocks and gravel in

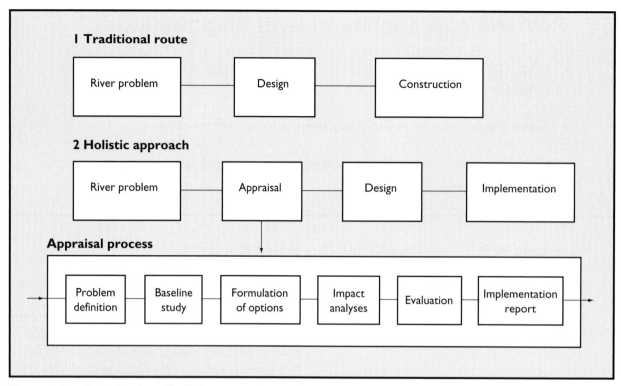

Figure 5.1   Traditional and holistic approaches to river management   Source: Brookes and Gregory, 1988.

the stream bed to restore stability and habitat following the river works.

- Retain river vegetation where possible or replant or reseed banks with native trees, plants and grasses to provide cover for wildlife and prevent bank erosion.

- Try to use natural vegetation as a means of bank protection and restrict the use of bank protection methods to the parts of the river channel suffering erosion.

- Only carry out clearing and snagging operations at localised points where significant blockages in the river are likely to cause flood problems.

- Only perform partial or selective weed cutting. In partial cutting at least 25 per cent of the vegetation cover should be left to conserve plants, invertebrates and fish. Selective cutting or clearance involves the removal of particular (problematical) plants.

- Time all operations carefully to avoid critical stages in the life cycles of the riverine fauna and flora.

In addition to these fundamental guidelines there are many detailed recommendations relating to the individual engineering techniques. Some of these are presented here.

5.2.1 Recommendations for realignment

Detailed recommendations have been reported by Brookes (1988, p. 194) relating to the planning, design, construction, clean-up phase and maintenance of realigned river channels, based on procedures carried out by the Oregon State Highways Department (after McClellan, 1974) and the guidance provided by Yearke (1971) and Brice (1981). However, the three main guidelines are as follows. First, prior to construction, the channel should be examined for about 1 km upstream of the proposed engineering works to assess the river's susceptibility to erosion and the need for subsequent erosion-control measures. Second, to prevent erosional problems, every effort should be made to approximate the shape of the natural channel through the realigned section, and slope increases should be kept to a minimum. If trapezoidal cross-sections are constructed, the bank slopes should be less than 2:1 to achieve stability. And third, the use of meandering alignments should always be considered in realignment schemes. Although they are more expensive to construct than straight channels, due to the greater excavation costs of dredging an asymmetric channel, the environmental benefits and reduced maintenance costs may offset increased construction costs over the life of the scheme. Well-designed meandering channels are more stable, provide a greater variety of flow conditions and aquatic habitat diversity, and have a better appearance than straightened rivers (Hey and Thorne, 1986). In the design of a stable meandering channel, the existing natural meander geometry and slope should be used as a guide.

5.2.2 Recommendations for resectioning

All resectioning operations should either adopt the principle of 'working from one bank' or they should alternate the channel works from one bank to the other. By working from one bank only, the vegetation and wildlife are left almost entirely untouched on the opposite bank, whereas alternating the location of channel works preserves the overall appearance of the river and avoids sensitive habitats, such as otter holts.

Resectioning should also avoid over-enlarging the channel. The excavation works should avoid both the creation of very deep pools, which serve as silt traps and preclude light from reaching the channel

bed, and excessive widening of the channel, because this reduces the depth of water in a channel for a given discharge and limits the area in which aquatic plants can successfully grow. Riffle–pool sequences should be preserved wherever possible to maintain a variety of flow conditions and morphological diversity in the channel because both help to promote habitat and species diversity. Unaltered areas should also be retained to serve as refuge areas which are very important in the biological recovery of channelised reaches. Finally, stands of aquatic plants should be preserved or created along channel margins because this also increases habitat diversity and promotes bank stability (Figure 5.2).

5.2.3 Recommendations for embankments

Traditionally, embankments have been constructed tight up against the watercourse, to maximise the use of every part of the floodplain, and riverside

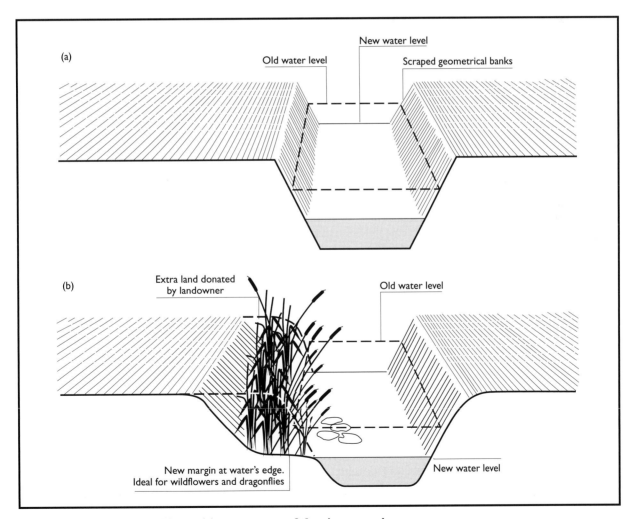

Figure 5.2   Sensitive and insensitive treatment of the river margin
(a) traditional trapezoidal section (b) a little extra land taken for a 'berm' which provides a waterside habitat for wild flowers and dragonflies
Source: Purseglove, 1989, p. 170.
Note: this is a design suitable for lowland channels but is unlikely to be appropriate for high-energy, upland streams.

50

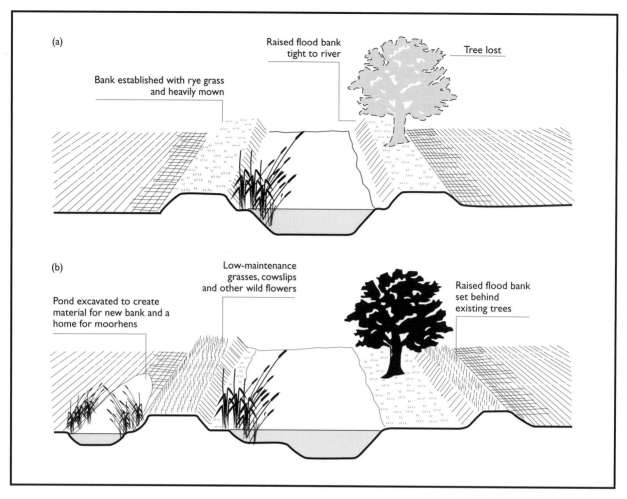

(a)

Raised flood bank
tight to river

Tree lost

Bank established with rye grass
and heavily mown

(b)

Low-maintenance
grasses, cowslips
and other wild flowers

Raised flood bank
set behind
existing trees

Pond excavated to create
material for new bank and a
home for moorhens

Figure 5.3   Raised flood banks beside the river
(a) Bad practice shows banks tight to the river and expensively mown   (b) Good practice shows a
more relaxed approach and a pond created in order to provide material to build the banks
Source: Purseglove, 1989, p. 182.

hedges and trees have been replaced with a cover
of closely mown grass (Figure 5.3a). It is only in
the last decade that embankments have been
designed, constructed and maintained with
environmental considerations in mind (Figure
5.3b), for example on the River Avon at
Birlingham in Worcestershire, England (see box).

Environmentally-sensitive flood banks are set back
from the immediate edge of the channel to allow
the development of a corridor for wildlife along the
river margin. There are also economic gains: the
embankments are shorter and, therefore, cheaper to
construct than embankments that follow a
meandering river; they don't have to be constructed so high to achieve the same flood storage;
and finally they are easier to maintain because they
are less liable to suffer from riverbank erosion. The
design also allows trees, shrubs and reed beds to be
retained or planted on the inside of a new flood
bank. Embankments should then be seeded with
herbs and slow-growing grasses which will reduce
maintenance costs.

**New flood banks built beside the River
Avon at Birlingham are an early
example of a revised construction
procedure. With full agreement from the
landowner, embankments were
constructed to allow a marsh to develop
between the normal water's edge and the
base of the river banks. The material for
the embankments was taken from one of
the farmer's fields and enabled a pond to
be created which was quickly colonised
by purple woodstrife. By avoiding the
high cost of importing soil for the flood
banks, the scheme made a saving of
£5,000 (at 1983 prices) and enhanced the
river environment at the same time. The
newly-formed habitat is home to snipe
and duck in winter and flowering rush
and meadowsweet grow in the summer
months.**

Source: Purseglove, 1989, pp. 181–5.

5.2.4 Recommendations for river bank protection and channel lining

Bank protection measures have traditionally been very damaging but their impacts can be substantially reduced if some simple recommendations are adopted (Henderson and Shields, 1984).

The most important consideration is to limit the length of bank protection and channel lining to the absolute minimum required for stabilisation. By studying the pattern of flow velocities in a river channel it is possible to locate places likely to suffer from erosion and to protect the river bank in those areas. Apart from the obvious economic advantages, selective protection also preserves part of the river environment. In Hawaii, a similar scheme has left short lengths of natural channel called 'rest stops' between the concrete-lined sections of some channelised rivers to permit fish migration in an otherwise unsuitable environment (Parrish *et al.*, 1978).

Environmental impacts can also be reduced by giving careful thought to the types of materials used for bank protection. Rigid linings, such as reinforced concrete and bagged cement, have the most damaging effect on the aquatic habitat and should be avoided. By contrast, riprap of cobble or rubble, gabions, gravel armouring, grasses, trees and shrubs are all better for the river fauna and flora and can be just as effective in preventing erosion.

Vegetation is proving very successful in reducing river bank erosion and is rapidly gaining acceptance and popularity amongst river managers. Vegetation can be used alone or in conjunction with structural protection (e.g. riprap) but to be effective it must become established before the next flood. Vegetation provides protection in two ways: by increasing the friction between the water and river bank which slows the water flow and reduces erosion; and by increasing the strength of the bank because the root systems of the trees and shrubs bind together the soil and stones in the river bank. One of the best materials for strengthening river banks is the blackberry and it has been employed successfully on two regraded rivers in the UK: the River Erewash in Nottinghamshire (1985) and the River Isbourne in Worcestershire (1982).

Another effective method of bank protection, particularly on wide rivers, is to use woven walls of living willow. Sharpened willow stakes can be driven straight into the base of an eroding bank, and smaller, more pliant withy stems can then be threaded horizontally between these vertical supports (Figure 5.4a). This technique of willow spiling was used on the fast-flowing River Meece, Staffordshire, England, in 1981 and by early summer the willows were green and growing. Bundles of willow can also be laid rather than being woven between the upright stakes. This technique is sometimes known as 'fiddling' or 'faggoting' and was carried out by Yorkshire Water Authority on the River Ure, England, in 1981 (Figure 5.4b).

In addition to providing bank protection, trees reduce sediment losses from the river bank and provide shade to prevent high water temperatures and excessive weed growth in the river during the summer. Strategically-placed plots of trees beside a river are better than thin lines of trees along a bank top, and trees planted at the confluence of tributary streams with the main river also enable birds and animals to travel safely along river corridors.

5.2.5 Recommendations for river training works

Dikes or groynes have been used to stabilise long lengths of rivers such as the Mississippi and Missouri and recent studies have also shown that for smaller rivers, dikes could be used to improve the habitat for fish and macro-invertebrates in channelised reaches. The important consideration is to design dike fields that do not fill with sediment. This can be achieved by varying the length and height of dikes or by cutting notches in them to allow water to flow through the dike at intermediate stages and prevent sediment build-up by regular scouring (Shields, 1983). A variety of notch widths, shapes and depths are recommended through a reach to provide spatial and temporal habitat diversity but notch width should not be so great that erosional damage occurs and notch depth should be chosen carefully since it affects the extent of scour downstream.

5.2.6 Recommendations for clearing and snagging

Clearing and snagging should only be carried out if the vegetation and debris in the channel pose a flood risk. Logs that are rooted, embedded or waterlogged in the channel or floodplain and are not obstructing the flow, should not be removed. Similarly, rooted trees should only be removed if they are dead or leaning over the channel at an angle of $30°$ or more and are likely to fall into the

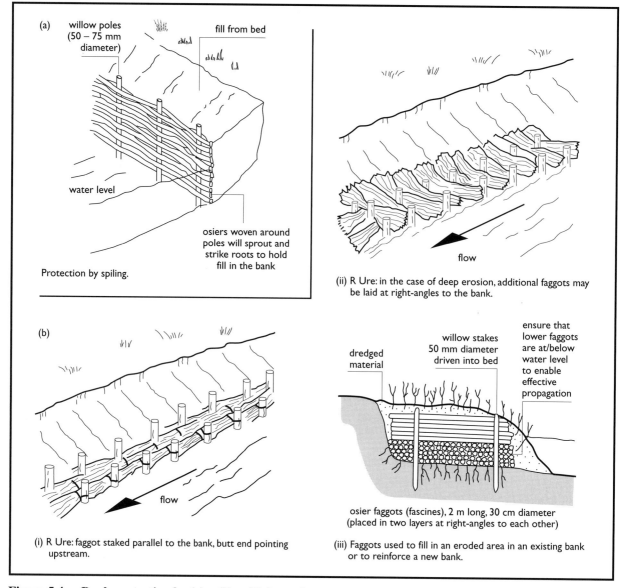

Figure 5.4   Bank protection by (a) spiling (b) faggoting
Source: RSPB, NRA & RSNC, 1994, pp. 288–9.

river and create a blockage. In situations when rooted trees need to be removed, they should be cut well above the base, leaving the roots and stumps undisturbed to preserve bank stability.

All clearing and snagging operations should be carried out by hand or with hand-operated equipment. If larger machinery is required, waterborne equipment is preferable since it reduces the overall environmental impact, particularly any damage to floodplain vegetation. Furthermore, all operations should try to work from one bank or alternate from bank to bank. To further reduce the impact on river wildlife, any animals removed during clearing and snagging (e.g. crayfish) should be washed from the dredged material and reinstated, and all disturbed bankside areas should be reseeded or replanted.

5.2.7 Recommendations for weed control

In managing river vegetation, it should always be remembered that the greater the variety of river flora, the greater the diversity of habitats in the river environment, and its wholesale removal can destabilise the river system. The sensitive management of river vegetation can be achieved by practising partial or selective weed cutting or by using shading techniques.

A key recommendation in partial cutting is to cut weeds along the fastest-flowing part of the river (thalweg) only. This preserves the marginal vegetation, which continues to provide food and shelter for macro-invertebrates and fish, and protects the river bank, while allowing the unhindered flow of water through the central part of the channel. Alternatively, selective cutting

Table 5.1   **Optimum shade for the management of lowland streams**

1. Light should be reduced to about half that in open river sections to reduce the standing crop of macrophytes by about a half. Shading to levels substantially below a half should not be undertaken because this will lead to the disappearance of aquatic plants together with associated loss of habitat and hiding places for fish and invertebrates. Trees and bushes need to be occasionally cut to prevent excessive shading.

2. On very small streams (about 2 m wide), stream banks should be left ungrazed by livestock, allowing herbaceous plants and marginal grasses to grow. Management is required every 3 to 5 years during the autumn to limit plant development. One bush every 30 m is acceptable to provide variety.

3. Larger streams (3–8 m) require bushes or small trees on the south bank or larger trees on the north bank if the river flow is from east to west.

4. Rivers greater than 15 m wide may require mature trees on the south bank.

Note: not all rivers flow from east to west; therefore each site needs to be considered individually to provide optimum shade.

Source: Brookes, 1988, p. 34 (after Dawson and Kern-Hansen, 1979).

allows the removal of problem plants such as filamentous algae while avoiding the cutting of aquatic weeds that are an integral part of the ecosystem.

An example of thoughtful weed cutting was carried out on the River Cary in Somerset, England, by Wessex Water Authority in 1980 in a way that removed the dominant and problematic bur reed but left smaller stands of scarcer plants, such as narrow-leafed water plantain and flowering rush, undamaged. The slower-growing plants were thus given a competitive advantage over the bur reed and weed cutting is now required less frequently. To implement this sympathetic river management, operators of weed-cutting machinery should be provided with books, identification cards and videos for the simple identification of different water weeds.

The use of shading to control aquatic vegetation is environmentally more acceptable than weed cutting and optimum shading conditions for lowland streams are summarised in Table 5.1. Although shading is a long-term method of management, because of the time needed for trees and large shrubs to become established, it has distinct advantages over other methods of weed control: shading creates a diversity of habitats; it is more economical and less damaging to the river environment than regular weed cutting; the overhanging and submerged vegetation provides a source of food for invertebrates; shade helps to maintain suitable water temperatures; and naturally shaded rivers are much more attractive than watercourses stripped of their vegetation.

5.3   Mitigation and enhancement techniques

In many existing or planned channelisation projects, it is possible to further reduce the long-term environmental impact by using one or more of the mitigation and enhancement techniques.

5.3.1 In-stream devices

These are structures that can be used to increase the rivers's habitat diversity by altering the river flow conditions, the channel morphology, or the substrate. They may be installed at any time after construction but their benefits will be greatest if they are installed immediately in any newly-designed channel.

Deflectors (Figure 5.5) function in a similar way to groynes in that they can direct river flows to remove sediment deposits and they can be used to narrow a channel. In streams in North Jutland, Denmark, deflectors have been installed to produce meandering thalwegs by placing them on alternate banks with a spacing of approximately 5 to 7 channel widths, which is the average pool–riffle spacing found in natural streams.

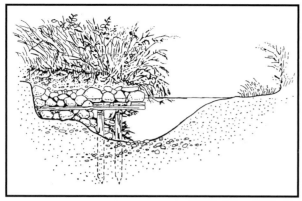

Figure 5.5   Cross-section showing deflector and bank cover device Source: Brookes, 1988, p. 213 (after White, 1968).

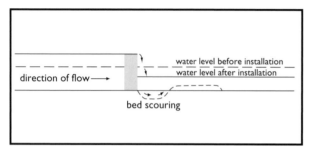

Figure 5.6   The effects of a low dam on streamflow and channel morphology
Source: Swales, 1982b.

Small weirs and low dams (Figure 5.6) can be used to diversify a river habitat by impounding a greater depth of water above the structure and by increasing the flow velocity downstream which eventually erodes a scour pool. The material eroded from this section will then be deposited further downstream as a riffle. These structures extend across the entire river channel, although some may have a notch cut in them to concentrate the flows in one particular location. Weirs can be constructed from logs, rocks, gabions or concrete but they must be firmly built into the river bed and banks if they are to be successful.

Cover devices can be used to provide shade and shelter for river fauna and flora. Rock-filled gabions can be fixed to the bed or banks of a channel and planted with vegetation (Figure 5.5), or interwoven willow branches can be allowed to float in the river to provide cover and shade.

Recreated margins of river vegetation can also be used to enhance a wide variety of river environments (Figure 5.7). In the River Anker in Nuneaton, margins of yellow iris and sedge were

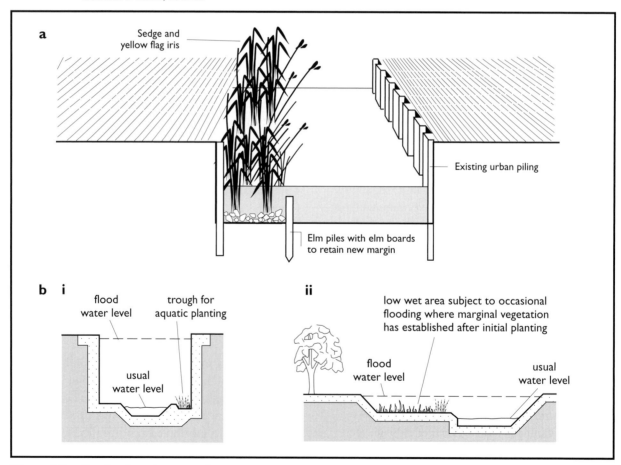

Figure 5.7   Replanting river margins
(a) Artificial margin established in an urban steel-sided river Source: Purseglove, 1989, p. 173
(b) Ford Brook, River Tame catchment, north of Birmingham Source: RSPB, NRA & RSNC, 1994, p. 347.

installed in the steel-sided channel and within one year further stands of water plants, providing cover and food for insect life, encouraged ducks back to this previously deserted urban watercourse (Figure 5.7a). In Ford Brook, part of the River Tame catchment north of Birmingham, a vertical-sided concrete channel was planted with soft rush, reed canary-grass, branched bur-reed and yellow flag (Figure 5.7bi) while the sections with berms were planted with yellow flag, soft rush, common reed, branched bur reed, purple loosestrife, water-mint, meadowsweet kingcup and ragged robin (Figure 5.7bii).

5.3.2 Artificial substrate

The replacement of natural river bed sediments following channelisation greatly assists the morphological and biological recovery of rivers. However, where natural river sediments have not been preserved, artificial materials, such as crushed rock, may be installed to improve the river habitat. On the River Ock in Oxfordshire (UK), for example, crushed limestone and flint gravels were installed over a bare clay river bed (Spillet and Armstrong, 1984). Regular surveys indicated a significant increase in invertebrate populations and improvements in the biological quality of the river at intervals of 4, 10 and 20 weeks after reinstatement. The limestone substrate supported a much higher invertebrate density than the clay bedrock and the rate of recolonisation was much faster in the enhanced area.

5.3.3 Pools and riffles

Pools and riffles can be constructed in both lined and unlined channelised streams to enhance the habitat for fish. In a channelised reach of the Olentangy River in Ohio (USA), for example, which had been enhanced with pools and riffles, the macro-invertebrate numbers and diversity were similar to those in natural streams; game fish were more abundant in the enhanced reach; and the numbers of non-game species were greater than in the natural area (Edwards et al., 1984).

The spacing of pool–riffle sequences is not critical in lined channels but for unlined channels an average spacing of 5 to 7 channel widths emulates natural conditions and allows the features to be self-maintaining. It is important to avoid completely regular spacing and to incorporate a meandering channel alignment in the overall design with riffles located in the straight river sections and pools at the bends.

5.4 Alternative river designs

5.4.1 Two-stage river channels

The two-stage river channel has proved to be an effective design for alleviating floods on some rivers and has fewer adverse impacts on the river environment than conventional techniques of channel enlargement. Very importantly, this design overcomes the problems of sedimentation and excessive water temperatures typical of many resectioned rivers. In the two-stage design normal river flows are confined to the original natural channel, or a newly constructed channel, whilst the flood flows are contained within a larger channel excavated out of the floodplain. Clearly, it is advantageous to retain the existing natural channel because the original substrate, bedforms and alignment are all preserved. However, if a new low-flow channel must be constructed, the morphological characteristics of the original channel should be copied as far as possible.

The channel excavated for the River Ray, Oxfordshire (UK), adopted a more conventional two-stage design (Figure 5.8) but more recently, a flexible two-stage channel was constructed for the River Roding flood alleviation scheme (Figure 5.9). The design is called 'flexible' because excavation of the second stage or flood channel alternates from bank to bank. This helps to avoid damage to sensitive river habitats and improves the morphological diversity of the river, as well as its appearance. Surveys of fish populations on the River Roding, Essex (UK), undertaken before and immediately after construction, showed that the scheme had not resulted in any serious changes to the type or overall biomass of fish in the river, probably because the original channel was left relatively undisturbed by the operations.

A flexible two-stage channel has also been constructed on the River Lugg, Herefordshire (UK). The meandering course of the river was retained over several kilometres and the land was excavated on the inside of the meander bends. This provided the material for building new, raised flood banks which were set well back on the floodplain (Figure 5.10).

The construction of two-stage channels is not a universal solution to the problem of providing environmentally-sensitive flood protection, however. While it works well for rivers like the Roding, which has a low sediment yield and resistant clay river banks, the design seems far less

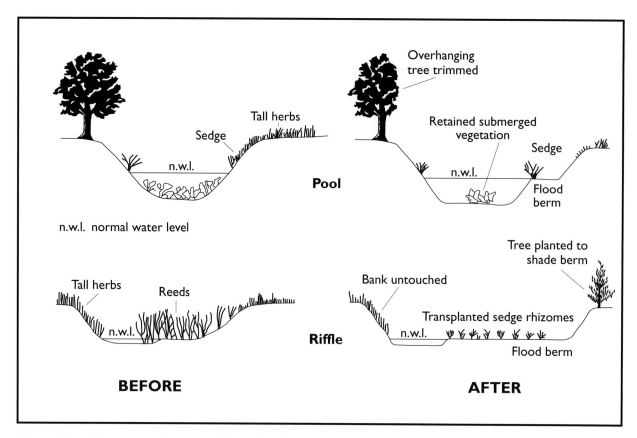

Figure 5.8 **Conventional two-stage channel design used for the River Ray near Bicester, Oxfordshire**
Source: Hinge and Hollis, 1980.

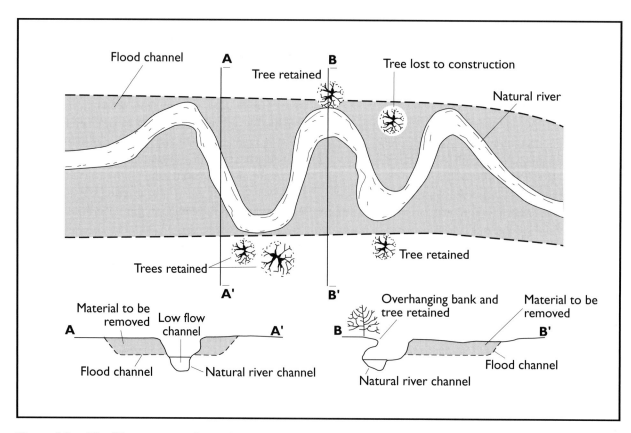

Figure 5.9 **Flexible two-stage channel design used for the River Roding, Essex**
Source: Keller and Brookes, 1984.

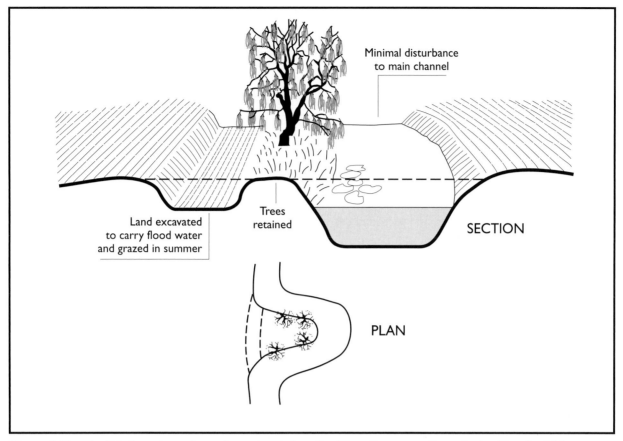

Figure 5.10   Flexible two-stage channel constructed on the River Lugg near Leominster, Herefordshire
Source: Purseglove, 1989, p. 180.

suited to a high sediment load and erodible banks, characteristics typical of many upland rivers.

5.4.2   Biotechnical engineering

The main application of bioengineering techniques in river management has been the use of living vegetation instead of, or in conjunction with, artificial materials such as stone revetments or gabions to provide an improved and more natural means of river bank protection. Although hailed as part of the new approach to river management in the UK and many other countries, bioengineering has been employed over the past 40 years in Austria and the former West Germany, and 30 years ago Seibert (1968) summarised how channel vegetation can be used to stabilise the channel bed, banks, floodplain and embankments (Figure 5.11).

Permanently submerged aquatic plants (Zone 1), such as watercrowfoot, pondweed and white water lily, protect the channel bed from erosion by reducing the water velocities near the channel bed.

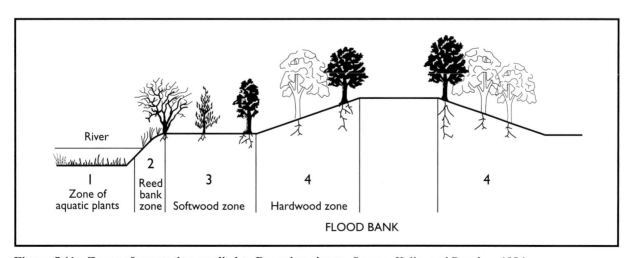

Figure 5.11   Zones of vegetation applied to Bavarian rivers   Source: Keller and Brookes, 1984.

Emergent plant species planted in the reed bank zone at the margins of a channel (Zone 2) possess roots, rhizomes and shoots which bind the soil in the channel banks under the water whilst the parts of the plants above the soil surface reduce the erosive force of the river currents and waves. Commonly used species include bulrushes, sedges and reed grass. Experimental work on the River Thames in Oxfordshire (UK) has shown the effectiveness of marginal plants in protecting against erosion caused by boat wash. The common reed (*Phragmites communis*) held the soil together more firmly than any other reed and provided the maximum degree of protection all year round.

In many cases some protection from inanimate materials is required until the vegetation becomes established. For example, wire netting stretched between upright wooden planks on the river banks can be filled with coarse gravel and then covered with reed clumps. When the planks are finally taken out, any gaps can be filled in with earth and fragments of reed clumps. A more sophisticated technique, but based on the same principles, has been recently carried out on the River Thames at Clifton Hampden (UK).

The roots of softwood trees (Zone 3) such as willows and alders also stabilise river banks when they are planted immediately adjacent to a channel. Tree roots can offer the best protection to a river bank but it is very important that the roots penetrate to the toe region of the bank because this is the most susceptible area and any erosion at that

Case Study: River Thames at Clifton Hampden, Oxfordshire.
Planting in association with Nicospan and Nicobags (RSPB, NRA and RSNC, 1994, p. 361).

Immediately downstream of Clifton Hampden Lock on the River Thames in Oxfordshire, bank repair and long-term protection works were carried out in 1988 using a combination of geotextiles and planting of emergent aquatic vegetation. Nicospan was used to retain the bank and planting was in Nicobags, large (2 m x 1 m x 0.5 m deep) non-degradable fabric bags filled with a mixture of silt and ballast dredged from the adjacent bed of the Thames. The bags were placed at the foot of the vertical bank to provide protection of the vulnerable toe region. Three 25 mm incisions were made in the bags and common reedmace and greater pond-sedge were planted into each of the incisions and firmly heeled down.

The scheme was appraised in 1993. The stability of the substrate resulting from the presence of the Nicobags has enabled the reed to spread from a sparse planting to a dense stand almost 30 m long and 1.5 m wide. Much of this reed bed developed from the natural spread of rhizomes, and shooting has taken place around the margins of the bags. The growth in front of the bags, combined with the growth of the planted reedmace, provides total vegetation cover at the water's edge. The reedmace and pond-sedge have been supplemented by the natural establishment of water-mint, great

willow herb and purple loosestrife. Now the reeds are so well established that they completely screen the Nicospan and accrete river sediments as they continue to spread as a fringe along the river. This continuous bed of reeds has also encouraged the breeding of sedge and reed warblers.

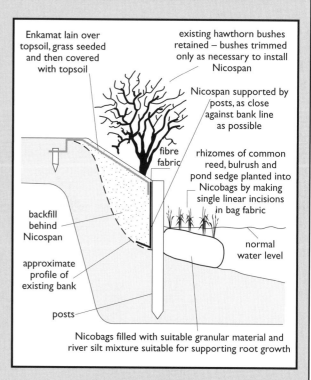

Figure 5.12 Planting in association with Nicospan and Nicobags on River Thames at Clifton Hampden Source: RSPB, NRA and RSNC, 1994, p. 361.

point increases the risk of tree collapse. It is also essential that the wooded growth on the river banks is continuous, especially around a bend where there is a risk of attack from high river flows.

A zone of hardwood trees (Zone 4) may also be established on the floodplain to protect embankments from erosion.

A further benefit of the vegetation zones is that they act as a 'buffer' between farmland and the river. The buffering capacity occurs as dissolved and particulate nutrients are removed by the plants and microbes in the strip. The creation of these riparian zones requires land to be 'set aside' along the length of the stream and a 10 m wide strip on each side of the channel is recommended because this allows several trees to dominate the buffer zone.

The ability of these narrow riparian zones to reduce the eutrophication of rivers and streams has been well documented, with existing research giving a reduction in nutrient concentration from 68 to 100 per cent depending on the initial nutrient levels and factors such as soil type and the width of the buffer strip. The benefits of buffer strips have been demonstrated by a research project on the River Leach in the Cotswolds (UK). The study by Nick Haycock, reported in *The New Rivers and Wildlife Handbook* (RSPB, NRA and RSNC, 1994, pp. 364–5), showed that for nitrate reduction in the river the only requirement is stable vegetation in the buffer strip and, although grass performs well, trees are generally better.

One objection by landowners to buffer strips is that the roots of woody vegetation will penetrate and clog tile drains as they pass from agricultural land under the buffer strip. To overcome this problem each tile drain could be replaced by a solid pipe. However, a better solution is to construct what are known as *horseshoe wetlands* (Figure 5.13). These are semi-circular shaped excavations at least 10 m wide and 8 m deep dug into the buffer strip to expose each tile drain as it enters the stream (Petersen *et al.*, 1992). These mini-wetlands allow the water carried by the drain to flow over a stretch of grasses and shrubs, before entering the stream. As well as improving the ecological diversity of river environments and increasing their flood storage potential, horseshoe wetlands help to reduce the flow of unwanted nutrients into rivers and streams.

Using a modest estimate of nitrogen uptake by wetlands of 750 kg ha^{-1} yr^{-1} this would give the horseshoe a nitrogen reduction value of 4 kg horseshoe^{-1} yr^{-1} (Petersen *et al.*, 1992). Thus, although each horseshoe is small, if a large number are constructed along the length of a stream, this will potentially have a large impact on nitrogen load. This impact will be most noticeable during the late autumn and early spring when tile drains are flowing which is significant because it is during peak runoff periods that most of the nitrogen and phosphorus leave the catchment.

The widespread application of biotechnical engineering techniques in river management may be assisted by farmers agreeing to take bankside

Figure 5.13 Basic schematic diagram of a riparian horseshoe wetland which will receive water from the tile drain and act as a zone of nutrient retention Source: Petersen *et al.*, 1992, p. 300.

areas out of production. In some situations it may even be possible to compensate farmers under the set-aside scheme whereas, in others, the buffer strips could be utilised to generate an alternative income, by growing trees for fuel (energy forests).

5.5 River restoration and rehabilitation

For channelised rivers that are no longer required to meet an engineering objective, such as flood alleviation or land drainage, there is the opportunity to return them to a more natural form and improve their conservation value. In some situations, a revised approach may achieve the flood alleviation objective which the traditional design has not been able to deliver. As it is rarely possible or even desirable to return a river exactly to its pre-channelisation conditions, river restoration is in fact often a process of rehabilitation or even creation. Some channelised rivers in high-energy environments may 'heal' naturally in the absence of maintenance but most rivers require some intervention to restore the channel features. The river fauna and flora will begin to recover once the channel morphology has been restored.

Most schemes require the restoration of river channel dimensions, cross-sectional shape, pattern and substrate, and there are many guiding principles including:

1. Straighten the channel and increase the slope as little as possible.

2. Promote bank stability by returning as many trees as possible; minimise channel reshaping; reseed disturbed areas promptly and install protective materials such as riprap very carefully and in selected locations.

3. Emulate nature in designing river environments (Figure 5.14). For example, channels can be designed with an asymmetric cross-section at river bends which allows the development of a point bar on the inside of each bend as found in natural channels.

Although restored rivers may be slightly less efficient in transporting water than conventionally engineered rivers, if properly designed they will be more stable, more productive (biologically) and require less maintenance. The period between reconversion of the channel and the time when the vegetation becomes fully established is a critical one in the success of the scheme, and regular

Definition of terms used to describe river restoration (after Brookes and Shields, 1996, p. 4)	
Full restoration	**The complete structural and functional return to a pre-disturbance state.**
Rehabilitation	**Partial return to a pre-disturbance structure or function.**
Enhancement	**Any improvement in environmental quality.**
Creation	**Development of a resource that did not exist previously at the site (i.e. creation of a new river design based on natural principles).**

inspection and maintenance are necessary to prevent failure.

5.5.1 Restoration of channel capacity

Rivers that have suffered aggradation can be restored to their former capacities by using the size of neighbouring natural channels unaffected by sedimentation to calculate the amount of excavation required. Alternatively, over-large channels which may have suffered degradation from a previous channelisation scheme can be narrowed to the size suggested by local natural streams, by incorporating a berm within the channel. On the River Lyde at Newham in Hampshire (UK), adjacent river reaches were identified as having the ideal natural symmetry and substrate, and the previously channelised reach required narrowing to an optimum width of 5–6 m. This was achieved by regrading the centre of the river and leaving a 3–4 m remnant of the existing channel as a berm at a higher level (Brookes, 1992).

Engineering reports and maps may also be available for consultation and can provide additional information on natural channel dimensions. The restoration or recreation of equilibrium (stable) river channel dimensions is a crucial first stage in any restoration scheme and should be the focus of more research.

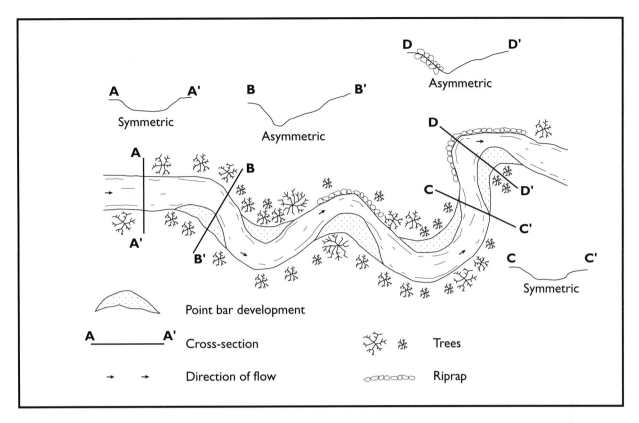

Figure 5.14 **A conceptual diagram to illustrate some of the main features of a more natural river design.**
Bank reinforcement through the use of riprap is confined to locations where bank erosion is greatest.
Elsewhere, vegetation provides protection.
Source: Keller and Brookes, 1984.

5.5.2 Restoration of channel substrate

Although the replacement of river sediment has been described as a mitigation technique it is also a necessary part of river restoration, especially for ecological reasons. For example, in streams in southern California, which were cleared in the late eighteenth and early nineteenth centuries for navigation, the habitat for salmonids has been recreated by restoring boulders and woody debris. These large-scale roughness elements change the distribution of hydraulic forces over a stream bed and cause the necessary scouring and sorting of fine sediment from gravel. Salmonid streams in Finland, such as the River Kuohunkijoki, damaged by dredging to allow boat traffic and timber floating, have also been restored by the recreation of spawning beds and nursery areas (Jutila, 1992).

5.5.3 Restoration of channel cross-sectional form

Asymmetric cross-sections lead to a more varied river habitat and are a principal aim of restoration. Experiments carried out by the geomorphologist Ed Keller on Gum Branch in Charlotte, North Carolina (USA) from 1974 have shown how the

manipulation of cross-sectional morphology caused areas of flow convergence and divergence in the river, which induced the stream to develop point bars in the desired locations along a 130 m reach of the channel (Keller, 1978). By varying the slopes of channel banks from 2:1 to 3:1 it is possible to induce a series of point bars and scour areas, similar to those found in natural streams, and thereby restore much of the natural river form. The reinstatement of pool–riffle sequences is also necessary for the restoration of gravel-bed rivers and the recovery of natural channel sinuosity.

5.5.4 Restoration of channel pattern

Only a few realigned rivers fully recover without intervention so there is considerable scope for restoration schemes 'putting the meanders back' into artificially straightened rivers. The most sensitive aspect of the reconversion often concerns negotiating the loss of floodplain with the landowner.

There are many examples of channel pattern restoration in Denmark and Germany. One of the first projects was the recreation of the former meandering course of the Wandse in Hamburg-Rahlstedt, Germany, in 1982 (Glitz, 1983) over a length of about 1 km. The officials of the Hamburg Water Authority were able to trace the previous wandering course of the Wandse because it showed up in adjacent fields as a damp depression colonised by kingcups, sedge and reed. One novel aspect of the restoration scheme was to leave as many of the abandoned straightened sections as possible as backwaters to allow the new water-courses to be rapidly colonised by plants and animals.

5.5.5 A building block model for river restoration

Clearly, individual channel features (sediments and morphology) should not be viewed independently in the restoration process, and Petersen *et al.* (1992) have advocated a 'building block' approach. This enables the river environment to be restored in a number of stages based on eight key 'building blocks' which allows flexibilty at a site (Figure 5.15). All, or any combination of the building blocks can be used to restore a stream depending on the local conditions. The model was devised for the design of small streams in agricultural areas in Sweden and is most appropriate for small catchments where it is easier to negotiate and fund land use change to enable restoration.

5.5.6 The UK River Restoration Project

The UK River Restoration Project (RRP) was born out of a series of discussions between enthusiastic professionals at a conference in 1990 entitled 'The Conservation and Management of Rivers'. In the last few years the group has expanded to bring together an even broader range of expertise and experience in conservation, geomorphology, engineering and biology. The RRP focuses on the practical application of restoration techniques to reverse the damage done in the past. It encourages others to assist in this process and promises to serve the environment and the requirements both of those whose livelihood and recreation are directly dependent upon rivers and of society in general.

The five main objectives of the RRP presented in its Business Plan in 1993 are to encourage the restoration of rivers by:

1. Setting up demonstration projects that apply state-of-the-art restoration techniques to the re-establishment of natural ecosystems in damaged river corridors.

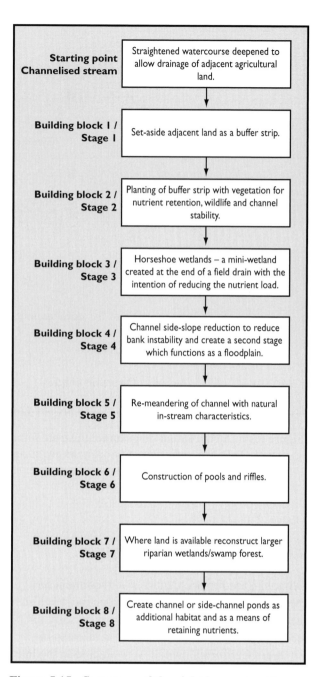

Figure 5.15 Summary of the eight key restoration measures (building blocks) which are proposed for use in the redesign of small streams
Source: based on information from Petersen *et al.*, 1992.

2. Understanding and measuring the effect of restoration work on nature conservation value, water quality, visual amenity, recreation and public perception.

3. Developing methods of establishing partnerships for structured collaborations between institutions that share a common aim to improve rivers but which have different powers, resources and responsibilities.

4. Providing a catalyst or focal point through which the practical development of other restoration schemes can be supported.

5. Disseminating knowledge about effective river restoration methods and techniques.

The river restoration research is being undertaken at three demonstration sites: the River Cole on the Oxfordshire / Wiltshire border to the north of Swindon (UK); the River Skerne, near Darlington (UK); and the River Brede in Denmark. The three pilot projects have a total budget of £500,000 from the EU LIFE Fund and are a joint venture between Sonderjyllands Amt and the National Environmental Research Institute in Denmark and seven organisations in the UK (Holmes, 1995; Holmes and Nielsen, 1998; Kronvang *et al.*, 1998; Vivash *et al.*, 1998). The main partners are English Nature, the Environment Agency, the Countryside Commission, the National Trust, Darlington Borough Council and Northumbrian Water Ltd, led by the non-profit-making River Restoration Project Ltd. In 1998 the RRP came to an end and a new River Restoration Centre was formed (see Appendix 2 for details).

In addition to the public bodies there are some voluntary bodies in the UK that have an interest in river management, for example the Lower Lea Project in East London and the Quaggy Waterways Action Group (QWAG) in South London.

5.5.7 Case studies

The Redhill Brook, Surrey, UK is one of a number of lowland streams in England which have under-gone rehabilitation since the mid-1980s. A 100 m length of this small watercourse had been artificially straightened and further realignment was planned in 1991 as part of a floodplain development project. In issuing a land drainage consent for this work the National Rivers Authority (now the Environment Agency) required the realigned section to be designed to reflect the characteristics of a natural lowland stream. This included creating a channel with varying channel cross-sections incorporating pools, riffles and point bars. Sediment was also reinstated which would not erode in a flood event that reached bankfull level (Brookes, 1996, pp. 246–7).

Repeated site visits were made in the five years following the implementation of the scheme to monitor its stability. It was noted that the recreated morphological features did remain *in situ* and there was little sediment movement or bank collapse. However, one problem which did arise, particularly in terms of the stream ecology, and which has been difficult to solve, has been the deposition of fine silt over the reinstated gravels.

The Stensbaek stream, Denmark. Denmark has the most impressive example of legislation which relates specifically to river restoration, and to some committed professionals to ensure that restoration initiatives go forward. The 1982 Watercourse Act provides powers for safeguarding the physical environment of streams by focusing on ecologically acceptable maintenance practices, and incorporates special provisions for stream restoration and the potential for financial support for such activities.

The re-creation between 1984 and 1985 of former sinuosity, cross-sectional dimensions, slope and substrate of a small straightened stream in Denmark is an example of full river restoration (Figure 5.16).

The Stensbaek stream has a drainage area of only 6 km² and the new channel was intended to replace an 800 m length of straightened channel which was severely degrading. The original course was determined from historical maps, from a field reconnaissance of depressions in the floodplain and from a comparison of naturally sinuous streams in neighbouring catchments with similar physical characteristics.

A series of trenches excavated in the floodplain enabled the approximate cross-sectional dimensions of the old channel to be determined, and these were checked by reference to natural reaches, with a similar drainage area, elsewhere in the catchment and in neighbouring basins. The trenches also provided information on the longitudinal oscillations associated with a pool–riffle sequence and on the substrate type.

A combination of grasses, for quick initial stabilisation, and woody species, for longer-term stability, were planted. Native species were obtained from the straightened channel before it was backfilled. The recreated course required stabilisation by riprap on the outside of bends before vegetation became established, and there was a ready supply of local assorted stones derived from glacial deposits. Stones were also stockpiled for later use to help prevent localised scouring,

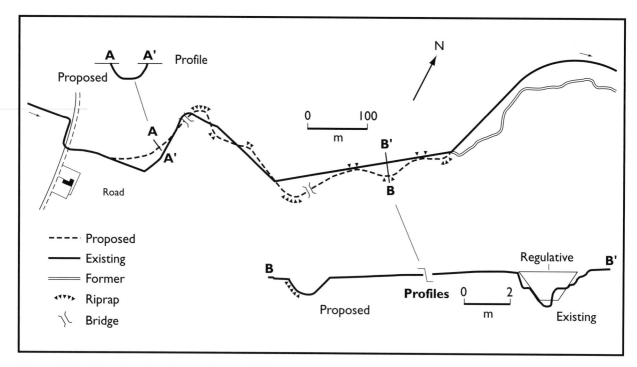

Figure 5.16 **Plan showing the position and dimensions of the restored course of the Stensbaek stream in southern Jutland, Denmark** Source: Brookes, 1987b.

particularly evident after high flows. Gravels were placed on the stream bed to recreate a natural layer which prevented downcutting. The new course restored morphologic and hydrologic diversity and the channel became successfully colonised by a variety of fauna and flora.

Speltach, an upland stream in south-west Germany. In 1985 the State Water Authorities started a programme for the rehabilitation of 15 sections of small streams all over the state of Baden-Württemberg, Germany (Figure 5.17). The programme was based on the *Leitbild Concept* which is a description of the desirable stream properties in relation to the stream's natural potential, regardless of its economic and political importance.

The Speltach was channelised in the 1930s as part of a scheme to improve agriculture. The former meanders were cut and the length of the stream course was shortened by an average of 7 per cent. At the same time, the bankfull discharge was increased to 13 m³ s⁻¹. The channel included a few weir structures but these were unable to prevent 40 cm of river bed erosion within 50 years. Local bank erosion also broadened the channel from an original average of 6 m up to 12 m in some sections.

The geomorphological study proposed that the 4.6 km stream section should be allowed to meander wherever possible, but measures to

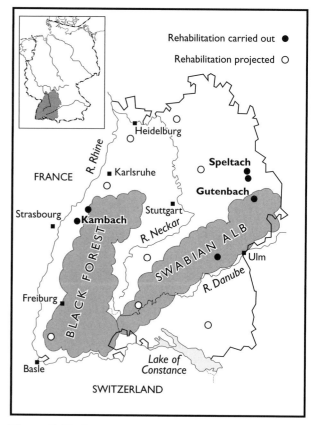

Figure 5.17 **Location of streams covered by the rehabilitation pilot programme in Baden-Württemberg, Germany** Source: Kern, 1992.

stabilise the stream bed should be used in sections with higher slopes. The channel rehabilitation was divided into three sections according to stream bank stability and bed erosion. In sections of no erosion, trees were planted above the average water level. In sections of mild erosion, the stream banks were regraded and several rows of trees were planted. The weir structures with vertical drops were changed to inclined ones to help fish migration. In areas that suffered severe erosion, the channel was broadened without stabilising the mid-channel bed. Single rocks and small islands were introduced to increase turbulence and the variety of habitats. Some heavily damaged reaches were armoured with rockfill and stream banks were regraded. Several rows of trees were planted along the channel and a 5 m riparian strip of land was created along both sides of the rehabilitated section.

In the long term, the recreation of a meandering channel pattern is essential to stabilise the Speltach, and more land will need to be reclaimed from the farmers.

5.6 Conclusions

Restoration and rehabilitation projects have now been attempted on small streams through to reaches of international rivers such as the Rhine, but relatively few documented examples exist. It is therefore difficult for river managers to make accurate recommendations or predictions about the likely success of restoration schemes, although a geomorphological assessment of an entire catchment can prioritise those reaches that are most likely to benefit from restoration or natural recovery. National databases, detailing the results of various restoration and rehabilitation proce-dures, would be of immense help to river managers and it is in this respect that the newly-formed River Restoration Centre will be of great benefit in the UK.

The costs of restoration also need to be carefully considered. The benefits of a sinuous river course, for example, need to be set against the financial loss of farmland and the costs of revegetation. In the USA, The Agricultural Wetlands Reserve Program was adopted as part of the Food, Agriculture, Conservation and Trade Act of 1990 and this initiative may help to fund the conversion of up to a million acres of croplands to wetlands, partly through a reduction of agricultural subsidies (National Research Council, 1992).

Further opportunities to restore rivers may also arise with future commercial or industrial developments, and the EA is now making recommendations for channel restoration to developers and landowners requiring Land Drainage Consent. If developers are planning to relocate a straightened watercourse then it may be possible to recreate a more natural course at the same time which could become an important feature of that development. Set-aside policies in the UK may also help to promote alternative river designs, allowing rivers more room and more areas for overbank flooding.

Points to consider and things to do

- What are the advantages of revised river management approaches? List the geomorphological, ecological and economic advantages separately.

- Summarise the arguments you might employ to persuade a farmer to take part of the floodplain out of intensive agricultural production.

- Are there any situations in which river restoration is not a viable option? Explain your answer.

- Suggest reasons why it may not be desirable to restore a river to its exact pre-channelisation state.

6 Managing river environments into the future

- *What are the long-term challenges of river management?*

- *How might the conflicting pressures of floodplain development and nature conservation be reconciled in the future?*

- *What are the implications of climate change for river management?*

As society faces the prospect of increasing population densities and global environmental change, the challenge of long-term, sustainable river management is huge. If this goal is to be achieved it is important for all decision-makers in river management to recognise:

- the integrated nature of river catchments;

- that 'rivers are meant to flood and must have room to move';

- that wetland areas are important in flood management and can be very productive environments too; and

- that changes in climate will have implications for the way river environments are managed.

In this concluding chapter we consider how these important issues can be addressed (and in some cases are being addressed) to enable a more sensitive and sustainable approach to managing river environments.

6.1 Integrated catchment management

We now know that river engineering in one part of a river basin will have consequences for the rest of the river environment because of the highly dynamic and interconnected nature of the fluvial system. Sensitive and sustainable management of the river environment can, therefore, only be achieved by adopting a more comprehensive, integrated and holistic approach in which all the competing uses of rivers are considered throughout the entire catchment (Figure 6.1). This is embodied in the principle of Integrated River Basin (or Catchment) Management (Kirby and White, 1994).

In New Zealand one of the principles of the 1989 Resource Management Bill is 'the maintenance of the natural, physical and cultural features which

give New Zealand its character, and the protection of them from inappropriate subdivision, use and development'. This Bill is enabling integrated, geographic resource management to be undertaken by 14 Regional Councils based on river catchments.

The same objectives can be achieved in the UK through co-operation between the Environment Agency and all river users. The National Rivers Authority (NRA) took a big step towards catchment management shortly after it was formed in 1989 by decreeing the formulation of catchment management plans (CMPs). These plans detail the catchment's potential and actual uses, environmental requirements for those uses, targets to direct management strategies and facilitate assessment of catchment management, and problems and conflicts within the catchment. The guidelines for production of these plans have been recently changed by the Environment Agency. They are now called LEAPs – Local Environment Agency Plans – because they include aspects of air quality and waste regulation.

Catchment planning can offer solutions to river management problems without the heavy reliance on structural river engineering. For example, non-structural flood alleviation could be achieved through managing land use to create a river corridor with floodwater storage, and controlling development and urban runoff within the catchment. Furthermore, an integrated outlook at the planning stage can lead to much more efficient catchment management and the cost savings can increase the range of management activities that become possible (Downs *et al.*, 1991).

For the world's largest rivers which flow through many countries, integrated basin management requires international co-operation. The River Nile is the world's longest river (6,825 km), its catchment area (3,000,000 km^2) covers one-tenth of Africa, and it requires integrated basin

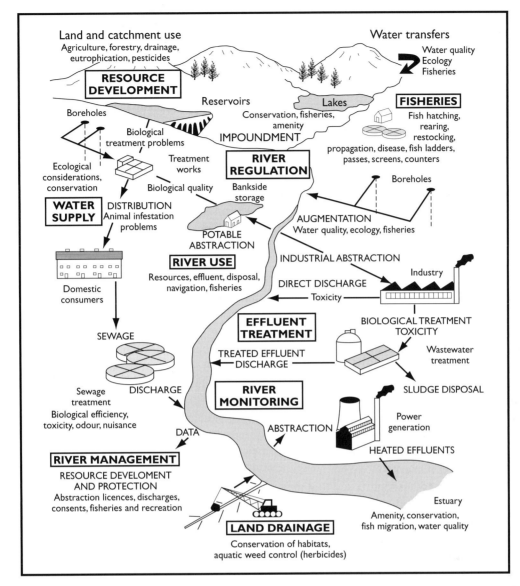

Figure 6.1   The water manager's view of the river basin
Source: Newson, 1997, p. xxix.

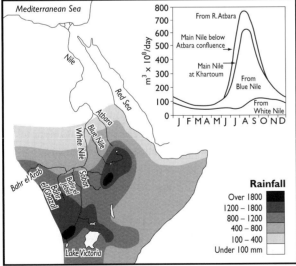

Figure 6.2   Nile basin annual rainfall and the Nile flood hydrograph, subdivided by contributing catchment
Source: Newson, 1997, p. 167.

management across nine nations' boundaries (Figure 6.2). The fundamental problem of managing the Nile is that whilst the six headwater nations on the White Nile (Uganda, Kenya, Rwanda, Burundi and Congo) are apparently amenable to joining a UN compact on the basin, they control only 14 per cent of the river flow. Ethiopia, on the other hand, is responsible for the 86 per cent from the Blue Nile, but it is politically, culturally and economically very distinct and refuses to join moves towards integrated basin management (Newson, 1997, pp.166–77).

The Nile desperately needs to substitute the principles of the International Law Associations' Helsinki Rules for the various treaties currently in use in the basin (Okidi, 1990). The most important Helsinki Rules comprise:

1. A fair distribution among the riparian countries.

2. This fair distribution to be decided by the following factors:

- the topography of the basin, in particular the size of the river's drainage area in each riparian state;
- the climatic conditions affecting the basin in general;
- the precedents about past utilisation of the waters of the basin, up to present-day usages;
- the economic and social needs of each basin state;
- the population factor;
- the comparative costs of alternative means of satisfying the economic and social needs of each basin state;
- the availability of other water resources to each basin state;
- the avoidance of undue waste and unnecessary damage to other riparian states.

The Ganges, like the Nile, is an international river basin with an area of 900,000 km² (see Figure 2.8, p. 19). One of the catchment's major problems is flooding in north India and Bangladesh. In the 1970s and early 1980s the Himalayan Degradation Hypothesis (Figure 6.3) emerged to explain the massive floods. The hypothesis proposed that the floods were the result of rapid and recent deforestation in the mountain headwaters of the Ganges and Brahmaputra rivers, which lie mostly in neighbouring Nepal. To cope with a trebling of population since the turn of the century, most of

the land available for cultivation in the Middle Mountains of Nepal (between 1,000 and 3,500 m) has suffered deforestation to create agricultural terraces. India and Bangladesh maintain that the outcome has been soil erosion, land degradation and increased downstream flooding.

However, information on deforestation rates, landsliding and changes in river discharge from a small number of case studies started to cast doubt on the degradation hypothesis, and in 1989 there was an urgent call for research into erosion processes (Ives and Messerli, 1989).

In response, an international and interdisciplinary research programme, 'Land Use, Soil Conservation and Water Resource Management Project in the Middle Hills of Nepal', commenced in 1991 to measure soil erosion and water pollution from chemical fertilisers. The soil erosion research was proposed and co-ordinated for the Royal Geographical Society by Rita Gardner, and the water pollution research was proposed and co-ordinated by Alan Jenkins for the Institute of Hydrology. The project is carried out jointly with the Central Soil Science Division of the Government of Nepal. The ultimate aim of the project is to improve the management of soil and water resources in Nepal through an improved understanding of both the physical processes and the farmers' land management practices. It is the first *integrated* study of hillslope and catchment erosion processes in the Middle Hills of Nepal, involving an integrated analysis of the hydrology, geomorphology, sedimentology, biogeography and agricultural systems in selected river catchments.

6.2   River corridors

A river corridor, streamway or floodway comprises the river and the adjacent land dependent on the river. Gardiner and Cole (1992, p. 398) have argued that the minimum river corridor is 'the area of land required for the river to achieve a natural meandering course with associated riparian habitats'. In practice, this corridor could be defined by the 1:100 year floodplain or be the strip of land bordering the river which is at least three times as wide as the lowest channel (Figure 6.4). In urban areas, defining a river corridor is more difficult but the ideal river corridor should still be designated, even if the floodplain is completely developed, so that future redevelopment will be obliged to recognise the restoration of the river corridor as a conservation principle. Within the USA,

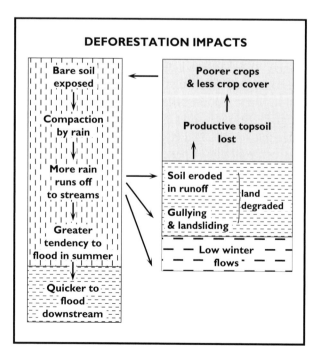

Figure 6.3   The Himalayan Degradation Hypothesis   Source: Gardner, 1994.

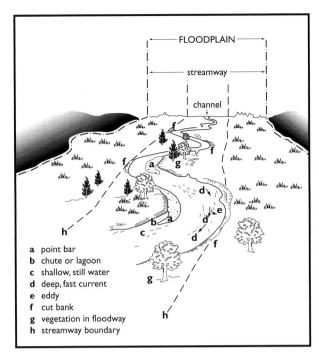

a point bar
b chute or lagoon
c shallow, still water
d deep, fast current
e eddy
f cut bank
g vegetation in floodway
h streamway boundary

Figure 6.4   The streamway concept
Source: Palmer, 1976.

communities must adopt a regulatory floodway to be eligible for the National Flood Insurance Program and developments within the floodway that increase the height of the 100-year flood over one foot are prohibited (Brookes *et al.*, 1996).

The benefits to be achieved by promoting river corridors are numerous. First, they are an environmentally-acceptable approach for managing floods and river channel change which avoids modifying the existing channel. The corridor protects open land for flood storage and provides room for the river to change its course. Rivers may take hundreds of years to migrate over the entire floodplain but individual meanders can completely change position in a few decades. The task of geomorphologists is to determine the width and location of a corridor that will accommodate a migrating meander belt. As well as preserving the river habitats this is a more economic solution in the longer term than attempting to confine the river to a single position by straightening and extensive bank protection. In Denmark, river corridors were suggested for artificially-straightened channels that were starting to meander again in the absence of maintenance (Brookes, 1984; 1987c). It offered a more economic and environmentally-acceptable solution than resorting to extensive engineering methods to restrain the rivers.

A second benefit is that river corridors conserve wetland habitats and preserve the morphological

and biological characteristics of the channel. Furthermore, the riverscape desired by conservationists is also that preferred by the public in their use of rivers for recreation and amenity. A questionnaire of river users (canoeists, anglers, rowers, walkers, and picnickers) on reaches of the rivers Wye, Stort, Exe, Colne, Aire and Goyt (UK) revealed that the public's ideal river environment included trees, a diverse vegetation and mature, sinuous rivers with natural channels and banks (House and Sangster, 1991).

And thirdly, river corridors will help to retain open land protected by Green Belt or other designations. Although there are many river reaches which have been designated SSSIs, AONBs and ESAs, the problem remains that only specific river sites are recognised for their conservation value and the intervening sections are allowed to deteriorate. In many instances the entire river from source to mouth is of sufficiently high nature conservation importance to merit notification as an SSSI, for example, the River Blythe in Worcestershire, the River Itchen in Hampshire and the River Avon in Wiltshire (UK). One challenge for river management in the future is to force recognition that the *entire river corridor* has existing or potential conservation interest and should be treated as a single unit subject to strict development control, with priority given to conservation, restoration and public access.

The success of river corridor approaches therefore depends on forward planning and strict control on development as part of an integrated approach to catchment management. Clearly, opposition to streamways exists in areas where any channel migration threatens property. But in the worst cases of house building on hard-to-defend floodplains, it might be worth considering the gradual abandonment of homes, with the government buying out home owners and demolishing the properties. In the London area, Thames Water assumed responsibility for flood alleviation following the demise of the Greater London Council, and its revised predictions about the amount of future development and its impact on flood flows has offered scope for a range of more sensitive engineering options, including river corridors. The overriding question, however, is whether the loss of land which river corridor schemes entail is a price worth paying for more environmentally-acceptable flood management.

6.3 Conservation and sustainable use of floodplain wetlands

Wetlands are the transitional areas between terrestrial and aquatic ecosystems and naturally border rivers and streams where they are known as floodplain wetlands. Although wetlands have appeared as hostile places in the past 'associated only with floods and disease' (Purseglove, 1989, p. 206), these riparian ecosystems should be recognised as a unique resource.

Wetland habitats are characterised by flowing water, high plant productivity and nutrient-rich conditions, and they provide the ideal conditions for a large diversity of vertebrate and plant species. In addition to the abundance of natural fauna and flora, wetlands can also support productive farming and perform very useful functions as natural storage reservoirs and buffer zones for pollutants.

In recent times, vast areas of wetlands have been destroyed by drainage to allow low-lying land to be developed for intensive farming or residential use. However, the production of surplus food, the problems of river pollution from fertilisers, environmental degradation caused by land drainage and channelisation, and the acknowledgement that the risk of flooding can never be totally eliminated, has called into question the economics of spending millions of pounds to protect areas where people do not need to live and which do not need to be farmed as intensively. While no one would suggest the complete abandonment of all floodplains and low-lying land to inundation by rivers, it does make economic and environmental sense for farmers to consider alternatives to high-input agriculture as sources of future income from their 'wetter land'. Sensitive management, rather than total neglect, is very much what conservationists want for wetland environments.

The following are some suggestions of alternative and sustainable uses of wetlands proposed by Purseglove (1989, pp. 92–138) and are based on the important natural functions of wetlands and the principles of good husbandry practised by early wetland farmers. Can you think of any other sustainable ways of using wetlands?

Nature reserves. The remaining unique wetland habitats and floodplain should be preserved and floodplains no longer required for agriculture could be restored. In October 1995, the World Wide Fund for Nature in Scotland (WWF Scotland) launched a 'Wild Rivers' campaign aimed at saving the last few remnants of Scotland's natural river environments; the only surviving ancient floodplain forest in Scotland is along the River Spey. The ecological consultant from the Forestry Authority is urging the formulation of a strategy for recreating some of Britain's floodplain forests in the next century following a successful initiative for the Danube (see case study, p. 71). These wetland reserves would provide refugia for wetland fauna and flora and in so doing would be both a 'living record of our landscape heritage' (Purseglove, 1989, p. 115) and a resource for the future.

Wicken Fen in Cambridgeshire (UK) offers a good example. It is a 245 ha remnant of the natural undrained Fens, now surrounded by intensively cultivated farmland, and is the oldest and most studied wetland reserve in England. The Fen has the appearance of a 'wet wood' but ecologists manage Wicken so that on a series of plots over the reserve every stage in the succession between total clearance and maximum tree cover is represented.

The vegetation on the various plots is maintained by careful mowing and cutting, and ranges in height from carpets of moss, through grass meadows, waist-high sedge, tall reed beds, and scrub thickets known as 'carrs', to the full height of mature woodland such as birch. Each of these stages of fen vegetation supports a different plant and animal community. The grass fields contain comfrey and hemp agrimony; the sedge is mixed with milk-parsley; the reed has a specialised bird life of harriers and bearded tit; the alder buckthorn in the scrub ensures the survival of brimstone butterflies; and the woodland provides a home for the sparrow-hawk, woodcock and long-eared owl. Even the pathways (or droves) vary from close-mown to foot-high swards, pink with orchids and ragged robin (Purseglove, 1989, p. 95).

The dykes at Wicken are also carefully managed to preserve the wetland fauna and flora. Regular maintenance is essential to create the most diverse ditch habitat and the dykes at Wicken, which currently support 17 species of dragonfly as well as water violet and yellow water-lily, depend for their biodiversity on a rotational winter dredge to prevent them becoming cleared.

Diversified, low input farming. A good piece of advice in selecting suitable farming practice for wetlands is offered by Purseglove (1989, p. 132):

Case Study: Recreating the natural floodplain forest of the Danube

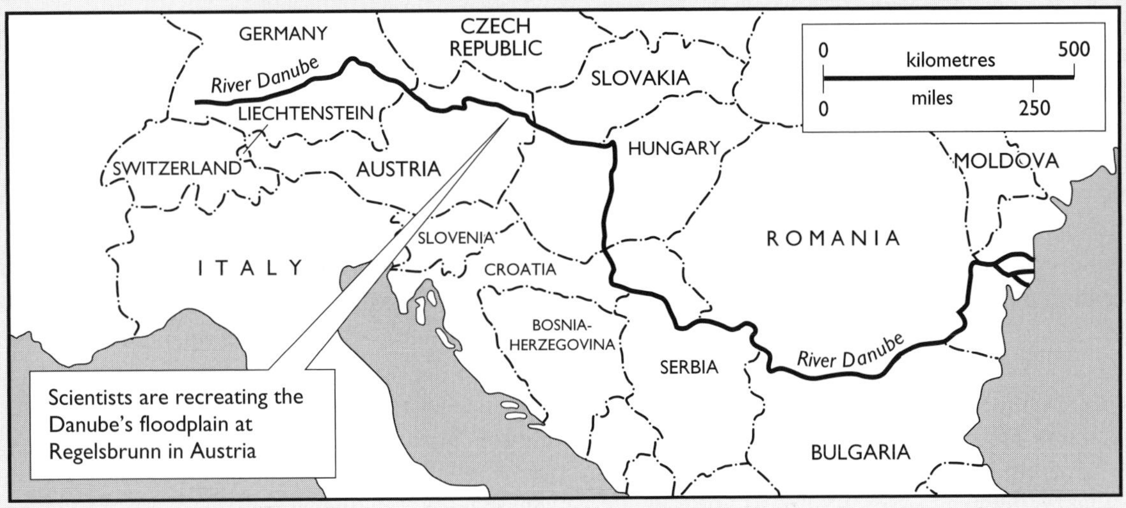

Scientists are recreating the Danube's floodplain at Regelsbrunn in Austria

Figure 6.5   The River Danube

On 11 October 1997, 2,200 acres of floodplain forest on the Danube at Regelsbrunn, Austria, was formally designated as a National Park. This is the only intact floodplain forest along the first 600 miles of the Danube. The restoration scheme, which includes breaching the embankments and opening the ox-bow lakes, reverses over a century of channelisation on the river. The aim is to preserve and enhance the few remaining areas where the Danube can flow naturally and interact with the floodplain. The scheme is part of the World Wide Fund for Nature (WWF)'s 'Green Danube' campaign. The organisation is also funding projects to restore floodplain forests in Germany, the Slovak and Czech republics, Hungary and Bulgaria.

There are many reasons why floodplain wetlands should be preserved or restored:

• Floodplain forests are important natural habitats and one of nature's most productive environments – as important as tropical rainforests.

• Floodplain forests are of huge recreational and economic value. The annual recreational value of the Regelsbrunn forest was estimated at £12m in 1992, based on the amount of money people were prepared to spend to travel there. The annual value of the timber, fish and animal feed produced in the area was estimated at over £3m. The study by the Technical University of Vienna concluded that the area had more economic value as a floodplain forest than it was ever likely to have as a producer of hydro-electric power.

• Floodplains are valuable as 'natural sewage works' filtering out pollutants such as nitrogen, phosphorus and pesticides. The WWF claims that the restoration of natural floodplains along the Danube could secure the safe supply of drinking water for 20 million people.

Source: 'Natural course of water and wood', report by Rob Edwards in *Scotland on Sunday*, 16 June 1996, p. 19.

'look at the land, and see what it has got naturally, which you can exploit'. A sustainable approach would be to farm the land to yield harvests appropriate to the limitations of local soils and topography and without the artificial prop of state subsidy. There is no doubt that wetlands can yield huge harvests of cereal per hectare but the cost of production can be enormous and the practice environmentally damaging. Alternatively, there are many other potential ways of farming wetlands such as using them for grazing, growing wetland fodder crops, as haymeadows, for forestry and harvesting other wetland fauna and flora (Table 6.1).

Flood control. Wetlands can be returned to natural floodplains and water storage systems by creating river corridors. This is particularly advantageous in areas where the conservation or restoration of floodplain wetlands is desirable and where flood protection of farmland or buildings is uneconomic.

Recreation and tourism. In 1985 the tourist industry in the UK had an annual turnover of around £14 billion, which was more than the whole of the agricultural sector; and in 1984 it created approximately 70,000 new jobs. One of the things which tourists come to England to see is the English countryside; wetlands are part of this landscape heritage and with careful management their wildlife can be enjoyed by tourists. Martin Mere, near Southport, is a wetland that has been restored after years as poor summer grazing; a farmyard there was used as a rubbish dump in the 1970s. The Mere is now managed by the Wildfowl Trust for its birdlife and attracts 185,000 visitors each year on average.

Such 'alternative' uses of wetlands do not provide an instant and unlimited economic solution for every riverside landowner, but they do suggest a more innovative and thoughtful approach to wetlands (Purseglove, 1989). A case study of the indigenous use of floodplain wetlands in West Africa (see pp. 73–74) also highlights the benefits of adopting a more sustainable and harmonious approach.

6.4 Managing the impacts of climate change

Climatic changes are known to have occurred during the whole time in which human beings have lived on the Earth but there is now great concern that human activity may be causing additional

Table 6.1 **Some valuable wetland resources**

Valeriana offincinalis
Tincture of valerian made from the roots of this plant is used as a sedative.

Hirudo medicinalis
The medicinal leech is one of 16 leeches native to the UK and has a long history of medical use. In modern medicine and research it is used as source of the anti-coagulant hirudin, as well as other potentially useful biochemicals. They are also increasingly used for controlling blood flow during micro-surgery, skin-grafting operations and treating 'cauliflower' ears in rugby players. Many of the leeches used in UK hospitals are collected in European wetlands.

Reed beds
Used for roof thatching. Reed beds created for thatching can also support populations of all the specialised rare birds of reed swamps. *Phragmites australis* (common reed) is a practical alternative to sewage treatment beds and can be used to treat slurry.

Rushes
The true bulrush *Scirpus lacustris* can be cut and used for chair seats or woven into rush matting for floor coverings. Cutting takes place in high summer and avoids the need for conventional river maintenance.

Source: Purseglove, 1989, p. 116–26.

global climatic changes mainly through effects on atmospheric quality and on the albedo of land masses (Tables 6.2 and 6.3). Increasing concentrations of 'greenhouse gases' in the atmosphere are thought to be causing increases in Earth surface temperatures, and there is evidence (e.g. Jones *et al.*, 1986) that over the past century the Earth's mean surface temperature has increased by 0.3–0.6°C; it is possible that it may increase by several more degrees during the next hundred years. The best available analytical tools predict (assuming current growth rates for emissions) a significant rise in worldwide equilibrium temperature, perhaps 1.5°C, by the middle of the next century (Figure 6.7).

Climatic changes will have far-reaching consequences for river environments and river management strategies in the coming decades and centuries. Global warming will result in changes in

Case Study: Indigenous use of floodplain wetlands in West Africa

The strongly seasonal flow patterns of many African rivers, with high flows in the wet season and low flows in the dry season, support wetlands of great ecological and economic significance. They include the floodplains along the Senegal, Niger and Logone-Chari system. Many of these wetlands support internationally important populations of wild animal and plant species but most also support substantial communities of people, who depend on their natural resources and the ecological and hydrological patterns that maintain them. Wetlands recharge aquifers, control flooding and produce a range of resources for human use. The Niger Inland Delta, for example, supports 550,000 people and in the dry season provides grazing for about one million cattle and two million sheep and goats. There are approximately 8,000 fishermen, and the Delta supports some 17,000 hectares of rice, half of the total area of rice in Mali. In dryland Africa, wetlands allow the production of surplus food and provide a sustainable income in both good and bad years for large numbers of people (Adams, 1993).

Within semi-arid Africa, wetlands also have a great economic and strategic importance out of all proportion to their size because their use is integrated closely with that of the surrounding drylands. In Sierra Leone, for example, the cultivation of swamp rice and dryland crops is carefully planned. Dryland and wetland crops require labour at different times of year and, by exploiting the two environments, farmers are able to regulate the labour supply and spread the risks of crop failure. Pastoralists also use wetlands seasonally, concentrating onto seasonally-flooded land as surrounding rangelands dry out. Thus a relatively small area of wetland provides support for grazing at critical times of year and supports this activity throughout the rest of the year over a much larger area. The Peul of the central Senegal Valley move away from the floodplain with their livestock in the wet season, but come back to farm when the floodwaters recede from the valley in the dry season. This integrative use of valley (wetland) and upland (dryland) environments to facilitate flood cropping, fishing and grazing is a basic feature of indigenous agriculture in West Africa (Adams, 1993).

However, the indigenous use of wetlands in West Africa is seriously threatened by agricultural intensification. Conflicts about shrinking floodplain resources are emerging in the floodplain of the Hadejia and Jama'are rivers in north-eastern Nigeria

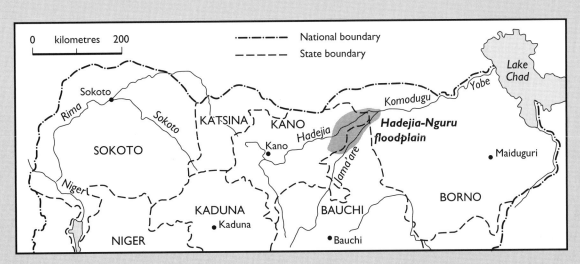

Figure 6.6   The location of the Hadejia-Jama'are floodplain   Source: Kimmage and Adams, 1992.

(Figure 6.6). The amount of flooding has declined in recent years because of drought and the construction of the Tiga Dam in the 1970s to supply irrigated land upstream. In 1950 the flooded area is estimated to have been 2,350 km^2. In 1986 it was 1,186 km^2 and in 1987 only 700 km^2. Shrinkage of the wetland has in turn been accompanied by demands for intensification of its use, particularly through the adoption of small irrigation pumps. Large irrigated wheat farms are being developed by 'elite' farmers in the floodplain since a ban on wheat imports has made such farming highly profitable. Land once open for cattle grazing in the dry season is now being cultivated, and there is a serious conflict between pastoralists and farmers.

Floodplains will have a key role to play in the development plans of West African states, but the development programmes and projects in these areas need to be sustainable. Sustainable development is directly concerned with increasing the living standards of the poor and it necessarily involves making sensible and effective use of natural ecosystems such that the benefits derived from them are optimised over long periods. It is important that people of these West African states recognise that the 'total economic value of a wetland's ecological functions, its services, and its resources may exceed the economic gains of converting the area to an alternative use such as wheat production' (Barbier, 1993).

Table 6.2   **Human influence on global climate**

Possible mechanisms:

Gas emissions
    CO_2 – industrial and agricultural
    methane
    chlorofluorocarbons (CFCs)
    nitrous oxide
    krypton 85
    water vapour
    miscellaneous trace gases

Aerosol generation

Thermal pollution

Albedo change
    dust addition to ice caps
    deforestation
    over-grazing

Extension of irrigation

Alteration of ocean currents by constricting straits

Diversion of fresh water into oceans

Source: Goudie, 1993, pp. 302–4.

precipitation, evapotranspiration and vegetation cover which will affect the operation of fluvial processes to varying degrees. Land use practices may change, which will have further consequences for the hydrological cycle. And predicted increases in the frequency and intensity of tropical storms (Emanuel, 1987) combined with sea-level rises will lead to even more severe flooding in countries like Bangladesh. The hydrological and water resource implications of global climatic change are huge, as stated by Birgitta Dahl, the Swedish Environment Minister (reported in Askew, 1991, p. 392):

> 'As to water conditions, impacts are to be feared on precipitation, evaporation, water storage in soil, snow, and glaciers, water temperature, water quality and the sea-level. These impacts will change the conditions for hydro-power production, agriculture, forestry, fishery, drinking-water supply, urban hydrological facilities and harbours and will of course influence the economy.'

However, the information for decision-making is extremely limited. A central problem is that hydrological behaviour varies considerably from year to year and this 'noise' may overwhelm the 'signal' from the long-term trend of global warming. Attempts to predict the impact of climatic change on rivers will require answers to a large number of difficult questions such as:

Table 6.3   **Estimated composite relative contributions of human activities to greenhouse warming**

| Activity | Gases (relative percentage contribution) | | | | | |
	CO_2	CH_4	CFCs	N_2O	Other	Total
Fossil fuel use	42	3		1.5		46.5
CFC use			25			25
Biomass burn	13	1		1		15
Paddy rice		3				3
Cattle		3				3
Nitrogen fertilisation				2		2
Landfills		1				1
Other				1.5	4	5.5
Total	55	11	25	6	4	101

Source: Stern *et al.*, 1992, p. 50.

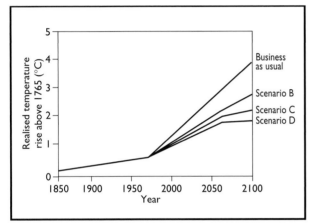

Figure 6.7   **Best-estimate projected increase in global mean temperature due to observed (1850–1990) and projected emissions of greenhouse gases under business-as-usual assumptions and resulting from Intergovernmental Panel on Climate Change scenarios B, C, D, which assume increasing levels of control emissions**
Source: Stern *et al.*, 1992, p.29.

- How will the temperature changes affect the patterns and amounts of precipitation in different regions and localities?

- How will runoff processes be affected by both the changing precipitation events and the vegetation and land use changes which are likely to result from a changing climate?

- How will the frequency and magnitude of flooding in rivers be affected by the climate and land use changes?

Climate models. Hydrologists use a number of

approaches to attempt to predict the impacts of global warming but the two main approaches are General Circulation Models (GCMs) and analogue models. GCMs simulate the large-scale features of the atmospheric circulation by solving the system of equations that govern atmospheric motion. With the advent of high-speed computers it became possible to solve numerically the complete system of basic equations that govern atmospheric motions (a typical run of one model year requires about three days of computer time). However, the real world is more complex than the GCMs designed to represent it and precipitation predictions especially are very unreliable at the regional scale, even for the present day.

Analogue models of global warming rely on studying recorded warm periods from recent times (modern analogues) or from much earlier times (palaeo-analogues), such as the Holocene optimum around 6,000 years ago or the Last Interglacial around 120,000 years ago. Different boundary conditions in the past, such as different atmospheric composition or Earth surface structure, may mean, however, that these past warm spells do not give a true picture of what can be expected under future global warming.

Climate predictions. The various GCMs indicate that warming will not occur in a regular and standard manner all over the world. There will be major differences between different regions so that rivers throughout the world will be affected in different ways. However, models do agree that there will be enhanced warming in higher latitudes in late autumn and winter. For example, a simulation by the United Kingdom Meteorological Office GCM (illustrated in Figure 6.8) suggests that in the northern hemisphere winter there will be a great swathe of land stretching from the north-eastern parts of North America to central Europe, the Arctic Ocean and Siberia, where warming may amount to as much as 6–12°C. Likewise the south polar regions show a comparable pattern in the southern hemisphere winter (June, July, August). In the same months, parts of the western USA and central Asia will also show pronounced enhancements in their temperatures. The various GCMs also all tend to suggest that warming in the tropics will be smaller than the global mean and will vary little with season, being typically 2–3°C (Goudie, 1993, pp. 354–355).

Simulations of the pattern of precipitation change are even more complex and show marked differences between different GCMs. However,

more recent models 'produce enhanced precipitation in high latitudes and the tropics throughout the year, and in mid-latitudes in winter' (Houghton *et al.*, 1990, p. 45). Changes in the dry tropics are generally small with both increases and decreases, though most models simulate an enhancement of precipitation associated with a strengthening of the south-west monsoon in Asia. The pattern predicted by one GCM, the UK Meteorological Office, is shown in Figure 6.9.

Predictions of precipitation change by Wigley *et al.* (1980), based on a study of warm analogue years in the period 1925–74 (Figure 6.10) and the reconstruction of Holocene Altithermal conditions (Figure 6.11), show less complex patterns than the GCM predictions. However, both analogue

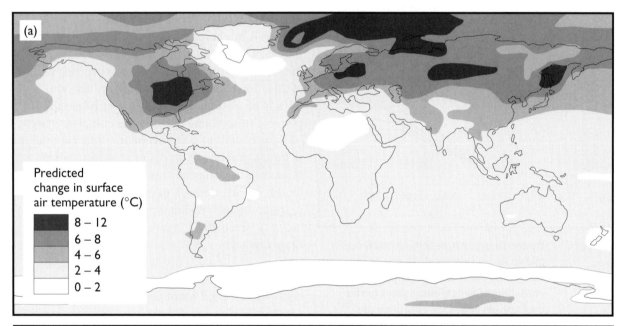

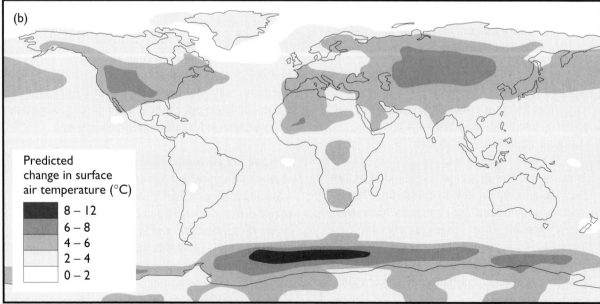

Figure 6.8   Changes in surface air temperature predicted for a doubling of carbon dioxide as simulated by the United Kingdom Meteorological Office GCM for (a) December, January and February and (b) June, July and August Source: Goudie, 1993, p. 355.

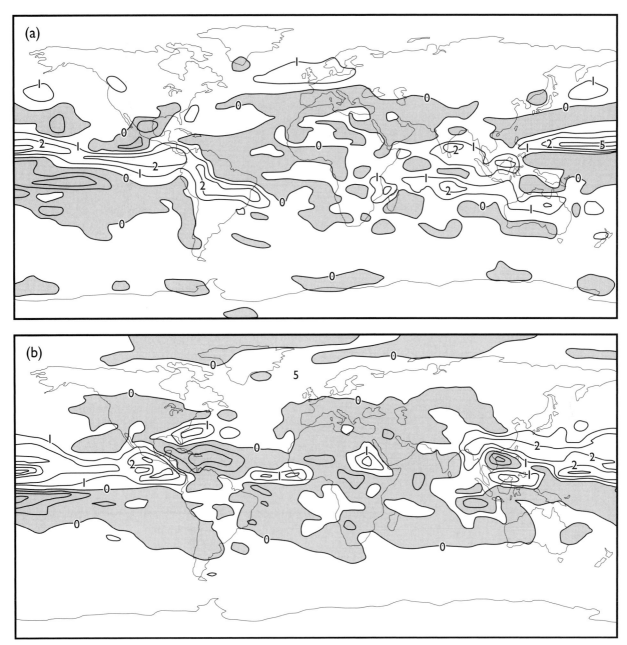

Figure 6.9 **Changes in precipitation predicted for a doubling of carbon dioxide as simulated by the United Kingdom Meteorological Office GCM for (a) December, January and February and (b) June, July and August. Contours are at +/– 0, 1, 2, 5 mm per day (areas of decrease are stippled)**
Source: Goudie, 1993, p. 356.

approaches tend to suggest that global warming will cause drier conditions in the huge agricultural region of the central USA. Predicted changes in precipitation over Europe under the enhanced greenhouse effect are shown in Figure 6.12, but this is based on the assumption that past correlations between temperature remain the same and can be used for predictions. How can scientists be sure that such assumptions are valid?

Combining the evidence from different sources can be problematic because there are often discrepancies in the results. One of the few attempts to predict future precipitation changes by combining evidence from palaeoclimates, modern

analogue data and GCMs is provided by Budyko and Izrael (1991). They believe that under conditions of marked warming both the mid-latitude and lower-latitude arid zones of the northern hemisphere will be wetter, whereas under conditions of less marked warming (by around 1°C) areas like the Sahara and Thar will become moister, but areas like the High Plains of the USA or the Steppes of the CIS will become drier (Figure 6.13).

Hydrological impacts. Changes in temperatures, precipitation quantities and the timing and form of precipitation will have highly important hydrological consequences. In areas affected by

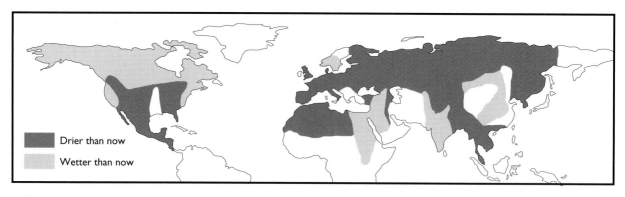

Figure 6.10 Mean annual precipitation changes from cold to warm years
Source: Goudie, 1993, p. 357 after Wigley *et al.*, 1980.

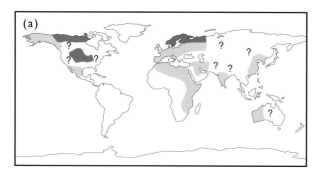

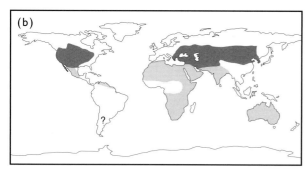

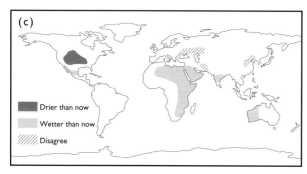

Figure 6.11 Estimates of surface moisture conditions during the Altithermal period *c.* 8000 to 5000 BP
(a) Kellogg, 1977 (b) Butzer, 1980 (c) Kellogg's (1982) attempt to compile regions of agreement and disagreement between (a) and (b)
Source: Goudie, 1993, p. 358.

snow. Furthermore, there would be an earlier and shorter spring snowmelt. The first of these two effects would cause greater winter rainfall and hence winter runoff, since less overall precipitation would enter snowpacks to be held over until spring snowmelt. The second effect would intensify spring runoff, leading to additional adverse consequences for both summer runoff levels and for spring and summer soil moisture levels (Goudie, 1993, p. 364). On the other hand, in high-latitude tundra environments warmer winters may cause more snow to fall, thereby creating increased runoff levels in the summer months (Barry, 1985). Indeed, Budyko (1982, p. 242) predicts that

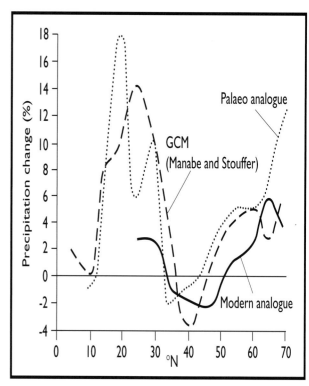

Figure 6.12 Changes in precipitation over Europe under the enhanced greenhouse effect
(assuming that recorded correlations between temperature and precipitation can be used for prediction)
Source: Newson, 1994, p. 7.

snowfall today, the changes may be especially marked. In a warmer world, there would be a tendency for a marked decrease to occur in the proportion of winter precipitation that falls as

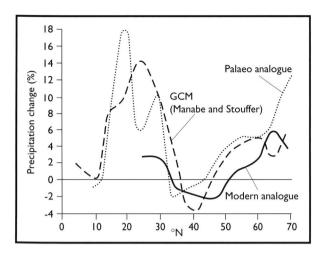

Figure 6.13 Relative changes in mean latitudinal precipitation on the continents of the northern hemisphere with 1°C higher mean surface temperature
Source: Budyko and Izrael, 1991.

because of increased precipitation (perhaps by as much as 500–600 mm y^{-1} in the tundra zone) runoff in Russia north of 58–60°N will increase by a factor of 2 to 3.

No less significant runoff changes may be anticipated for semi-arid environments, such as the south-west USA. For example, Revelle and Waggoner (1983) suggest that in the event of there being a 2°C rise in temperature and a 10 per cent reduction in precipitation, water supplies would be diminished by 76 per cent in the Rio Grande region and by 40 per cent in the Upper Colorado. Table 6.4 demonstrates that a 2°C rise in temperature would be most serious for water supplies and runoff in those regions where the mean annual precipitation is less than about 400 mm y^{-1}.

For the UK, Palutikov (1987) has predicted a general increase in wetness for the north of England but reduced river flows in southern England (Figure 6.14) based on analogues of past cool and warm periods with the climatic database of the UK. This pattern exacerbates the already rising demand for water resources in the south where summer drought could already easily become the norm.

Another analogue approach has been used by Macklin and Lewin (1993) to attempt to answer questions about likely river behaviour in the future. They studied river dynamics in the UK over the last 10,000 years. This research has shown that changes in the fluvial system over such time scales are mainly due to climate but that land use plays an important role in modifying the response. However, the impact of human culture is now much more widespread than at any other stage of the Holocene, and the land use factor may be much more significant in controlling future river changes.

Beven (1993) also acknowledges the difficulty of separating the effects of climate warming from the effects of continuing land use change in an attempt to assess likely future changes in river flooding in Britain. He argues that since a warmer Britain may also be wetter, at least seasonally, then it might be expected that the frequency of flood events of a given magnitude may increase. From an analysis of historical data it is not clear, however, whether the magnitudes of the most extreme events will also increase. For example, a study by Walsh *et al.* (1982) suggests that there have been periods of more frequent flooding in Wales in the last century but without any evidence for significantly larger floods.

Table 6.4   **Approximate percentage decrease in runoff for a 2°C increase in temperature**

Initial temperature (°C)	*Precipitation (mm y^{-1})*					
	200	*300*	*400*	*500*	*600*	*700*
−2	26	20	19	17	17	14
0	30	23	23	19	17	16
2	39	30	24	19	17	16
4	47	35	25	20	17	16
6	100	35	30	21	17	16
8		53	31	22	20	16
10		100	34	22	22	16
12			47	32	22	19
14			100	38	23	19

Source: data from Revelle and Waggoner, 1983, in Goudie, 1993, p. 365.

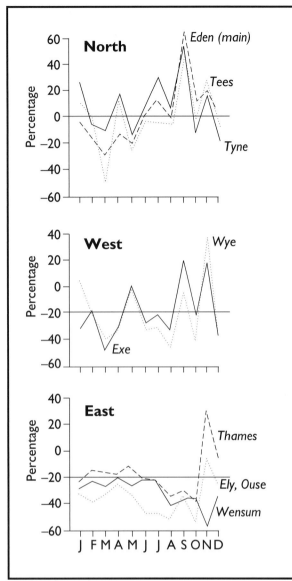

Figure 6.14 Models of monthly river flows for the Eden, Tees, Tyne, Wye, Exe, Thames, Ely, Ouse and Wensum (after Palutikov, 1987)   Source: Newson, 1992, p. 237.

Scientists at the Institute of Hydrology (Arnell *et al.*, 1990) have studied the impact of climatic variability and change on river flow regimes in the UK, but there has been no attempt to define possible changes in short-term aspects of flow regime such as floods because estimates of future climate are currently unknown. The research set out to answer two main groups of questions:

1. How have river flow regimes varied between years in the UK in the recent past, and what catchment and climate characteristics control this variability? Are extreme events such as floods and droughts distributed randomly through time, or do they tend to cluster? What is the long-term 'significance' of the various extreme hydrological events experienced during the 1970s and 1980s?

2. How might river flow characteristics change in the UK with global warming? What properties of a catchment will influence the sensitivity of flows to climate change?

There were four main conclusions to the research.

First, the variability in river flow characteristics between years is related to variations in rainfall and is generally larger.

Second, extreme events such as droughts and floods tend to cluster in time, and similar patterns have been observed across the whole of northern and western Europe (Arnell, 1989; Gustard *et al.*, 1989). While seasonal rainfall totals across different regions of England and Wales are closely correlated with circulation types (Jones and Wigley, 1988) there is no full explanation of why groups of years with particular dominant circulation patterns appear to cluster. A partial answer may come from Fraedrich's (1990) study showing a link between climate in western Europe and the El Niño phenomenon. There is the possibility, therefore, that clusters in European climate may be associated with multi-year patterns observed in West Africa or the Pacific Coast of South America.

Third, the hypothesis that there have been an unusually large number of 'extreme' events in the 1980s has not been supported. It has been shown that average annual rainfall and runoff was higher in the 1980s than in the 1970s but there are many examples of periods that seemed to show an increase in the number of extreme events but which were followed by a return to more average conditions. The hydrological characteristics of the 1980s cannot therefore be used to infer that global warming has begun to have an effect; they equally cannot be used to dismiss the possibility of future warming. What the results do indicate is that any assessments of hydrological characteristics or water resources potential based on a short record may turn out to be very inaccurate over the longer term.

And fourthly, different catchments show different degrees of variability between years and this is related to climatic variability and differences in catchment characteristics. The implication for river management is that the greatest variability is found in highly-responsive catchments with low runoff relative to rainfall.

Predictions of the impact of climatic change on riverine flooding depend very heavily on the accuracy of predictions of precipitation changes and, to a lesser extent, changes in evapotranspiration. For a scenario of a warmer and wetter Britain it is impossible to say little more than that the frequency of flood-producing rainfalls may increase, particularly in the winter and spring periods. In summer, any increase in rainfall is likely to be moderated by higher soil moisture deficits resulting from increased evapotranspiration rates. A warmer and wetter Britain may consequently be more prone to flooding, with greater frequency if not, on average, more extreme flood peaks. This has important implications for the management of flooding and river channel change. Increased flood frequencies may result in more erosion by rivers and the need for improved bank protection. There may also be a need for greater controls on land uses that might increase runoff, such as urban development (if there isn't adequate storage in the river basin) and better floodplain zoning regulations to curb new development on land sensitive to flooding.

6.5 'A reverence for rivers': principles of good river management

At a time when many of the ill-effects of traditional river engineering were becoming well-known, Luna Leopold (1977) wrote of the need for 'a reverence for rivers'. In the last two decades a more sustainable and environmentally-sensitive approach has emerged with better decision-making, better river designs and better working practices. This more 'reverent' approach has arisen from changes in river legislation, from knowledge gained about the impacts of channelisation and from a greater understanding of the behaviour of river systems. The challenge for sustainable river management includes 'improving the physical condition of watercourses to provide a diversity of habitats, reducing nutrient emissions to limit eutrophication and re-establishing the self-purification capacity of rivers' (Brookes and Shields, 1996a, p. 386).

This *Update* has tried to provide an insight into the issues and challenges of managing river environments and to show how policies and practices in river management have developed and may continue to develop in the future.

The fundamental task is to try to reconcile the often conflicting pressures of nature conservation and various land use activities with management of floods and river channel changes. By following the basic principles of good river management this may be an attainable goal:

- work with nature not against it and emulate nature in river channel designs;

- adopt river designs and working practices that are known to have the least damaging impact on the environment;

- always apply the principles of sustainable development;

- adopt integrated, catchment-wide planning;

- employ a detailed appraisal process and consult widely, considering all environmental issues alongside the engineering and economic objectives;

and

- always carry out post-project appraisal so that knowledge about the impacts of river management continues to grow.

Points to consider and things to do

- What are the benefits of integrated river basin management? Can you envisage any difficulties with attempts to implement catchment-wide planning?

- Are river corridors a universal solution to the problems of managing river environments? Explain your answer.

- To what extent do you consider some of the new approaches in wetland management are simply a return to much older practices?

- What are the implications of the predicted global and regional climate changes for river management? With reference to the climate scenarios, briefly outline the problems of planning for possible global climate change in the context of river management in *one* named developed country and *one* named developing country.

82

Appendix 1 Information about the Environment Agency (England & Wales) and the Scottish Environment Protection Agency

The work of the Environment Agency

The EA's work is divided into seven main functions:

1. **Flood Defence** has the role of protecting people and the developed environment from flooding by providing effective defences and protection of floodplains. Safeguarding life is its highest priority and to meet this aim it provides a flood forecasting and warning service. Flood defence also has an aim to protect and enhance the natural environment by promoting works that are sustainable and which work with nature.

2. **Water Resources**. This function comprises the conservation, redistribution and augmentation of surface and groundwater supplies. It includes the powers to encourage water conservation, to promote transfer schemes and to balance the needs of water users and the environment by issuing licences for users to abstract water from rivers and boreholes.

3. **Pollution Control**. This includes:

   Integrated Pollution Control (IPC) regulating the most polluting, or technologically complex, industrial and other processes in air, on land or in water.

   Water quality and pollution control which prevents and controls pollution and monitors the quality of rivers, estuaries and coastal waters.

   Radioactive substances – regulating the disposal of radioactive material, including that from licensed nuclear sites, and regulating the accumulation, storage and use of radioactive materials, except from licensed sites.

   Waste regulation – setting consistent standards for waste management practice to regulate the treatment, storage, movement and disposal of controlled waste. The Agency also has a requirement to register and monitor those who produce waste, imposing obligations to re-use, recover or recycle products and materials.

   Reporting on the extent of contaminated land and contributing to its management (primarily undertaken by local authorities).

   Abandoned mine operators are also required to work with the Agency so that steps can be taken to prevent minewater pollution in the future.

4. **Fisheries**. The Agency is responsible for maintaining, improving and developing fisheries. This is achieved through licensing, regulation and enforcement schemes which cover salmon, sea trout, non-migratory trout, coarse and eel fisheries; by improving the habitat and fish stocks; and by providing advice to fishery owners.

5. **Navigation**. The EA is responsible for managing and improving over 800 km of inland waterways, the Harbour of Rye and Dee Estuary. The aim is to make these resources widely available to the public for water- or land-based recreational use.

6. **Recreation**. Over 1,000 sites under EA control are managed for recreation. The Agency also has a general duty to promote the recreational use of water and land throughout England and Wales.

7. **Conservation**. In fulfilling all its functions the EA is required to contribute to the conservation of nature, landscape and archaeological heritage. It also has a regard to conserving and enhancing flora, fauna, geological or physiographical features when carrying out its pollution control functions, and a duty to further conservation when carrying out other functions. The Agency also has a duty generally to promote the conservation of flora and fauna dependent on the aquatic environment.

Source: Environment Agency, 1996a.

How to contact the Environment Agency:

Head Office
Rio House, Waterside Drive, Aztec West, Almondsbury, Bristol BS32 4UD
Tel: 01454 624400 Fax: 01454 624409

Email: enquiries@environment-agency.gov.uk

Web site: http://www.environment-agency.gov.uk

How to contact the Scottish Environment Protection Agency:

Head Office
2 Erskine Court, Castle Business Park, Stirling FK9 4TR
Tel: 01786 457700 Fax: 01786 446885

Web site: http://www.sepa.org.uk

Appendix 2   The River Restoration Centre (RRC)

The RRC was established in 1998 to build on the expertise gained from the River Restoration Project's Demonstration sites on the Rivers Cole and Skerne. It is a founder member of the European Centre for River Restoration (ECRR). The RRC is a non-profit-making organisation and will assemble and manage a UK database and information network, detailing river restoration schemes and techniques, which will allow impartial advice to be offered to practitioners and scientists involved in river restoration.

Information on the services of RRC can be obtained from:

Martin Janes
Centre Manager
River Restoration Centre
Silsoe Campus, Silsoe
Beds MK45 4DT

Tel/fax: 01525 863341

Email: rrc@cranfield.ac.uk

Web site: http://www.qest.demon.co.uk/rrc/rrc.htm

Bibliography

Acheson, A. R. (1968) *River Control and Drainage in New Zealand*. Ministry of Works: Wellington North, New Zealand.

Adams, W. M. (1993) 'Indigenous use of wetlands and sustainable development in West Africa'. *The Geographical Journal*, 159 (2), 209–218.

American Water Resources Association (1972) 'Trends and commentary'. *The Water Resources Newsletter*, 7 (4).

Arnell, N. W. (1989) 'Changing frequency of extreme hydrological events in northern and western Europe'. *FRIENDS in Hydrology. Institute of Hydrology Report No. 187*, 237–249. Institute of Hydrology, Wallingford.

Arnell, N. W., Brown, R. P. C. and Reynard, N. S. (1990) 'Impact of climatic variability and change on river flow regimes in the UK'. *Institute of Hydrology Report No. 107*. Institute of Hydrology, Wallingford.

Arner, D. H., Robinette, H. R., Frasier, J. E. and Gray, M. H. (1975) 'Report on effects of channelisation modification on the Luxapalila River'. *Symposium on Stream Channel Modification*. Harrisonburg, VA, pp. 77–96.

Arner, D. H., Robinette, H. R., Frasier, J. E. and Gray, M. H. (1976) *Effects of Channelization of the Luxapalila River on Fish, Aquatic Invertebrates, Water Quality and Fur Bearers*. Report No. FWS/OBS-76/08, Office of Biological Services, Fish and Wildlife Service, US Department of the Interior, Washington DC.

Ashworth, P. J. and Ferguson, R. I. (1986) 'Interrelationships of channel processes, changes and sediments in a proglacial braided river'. *Geografiska Annaler*, 68A, 361–371.

Askew, A. J. (1991) 'Climate and water: a call for international action'. *Hydrological Sciences Journal*, 36 (4), 391–404.

Baker, V. R. (1977) 'Stream-channel response to floods, with examples from central Texas'. *Bulletin of the Geological Society of America*, 88, 1057–1071.

Barbier, E. B. (1993) 'Sustainable use of wetlands. Valuing tropical wetland benefits: economic methodologies and applications'. *The Geographical Journal*, 159 (1), 22–32.

Barry, R. G. (1985) 'The cryosphere and climate change'. In: M. C. MacCraken and F. M. Luther (editors), *Detecting the Climatic Effects of Increasing Carbon Dioxide*. Washington, DC: US Department of Energy, 111–148.

Berz, G. (1992) 'Munich Re's list of major natural disasters in 1990'. *Natural Hazards*, 5, 95–102.

Beven, K. (1993) 'Riverine flooding in a warmer Britain'. *The Geographical Journal* 159, 157–161.

Bree, T. and Cunnane, C. (1980) 'The effect of arterial drainage on flood magnitude'. In: *Project 5.1 of the International Hydrological Programme. Casebook of methods of computation of quantitative changes in the hydrological regime of river basins due to human activities*. UNESCO, 116–126.

Brice, J. C. 1981 *Stability of Relocated Stream Channels*. Technical Report No. FHWA/RD-80/158, Federal Highways Administration, US Department of Transportation, Washington, DC.

Briggs, D. and Smithson, P. (1985) *Fundamentals of Physical Geography*. Unwin Hyman: London.

British Hydrological Society (1994) 'The Maidenhead, Windsor and Eton flood relief scheme'. *Circulation*, 43, 3–4.

Brookes, A. (1983) 'River channelization in England and Wales: downstream consequences for the channel morphology and aquatic vegetation'. Unpublished PhD thesis, University of Southampton, Southampton, UK.

Brookes, A. (1984) *Recommendations Bearing on the Sinuosity of Danish Stream Channels – consequences of realignment, spatial extent of natural channels, processes and techniques of natural and induced restoration*. Technical Report No. 6. Freshwater Laboratory, National Agency of Environmental Protection, Silkeborg, Denmark.

Brookes, A. (1986) 'Response of aquatic vegetation to sedimentation downstream from channelisation works in England and Wales'. *Biological Conservation*, 38, 351–367.

Brookes, A. (1987a) 'Recovery and adjustment of aquatic vegetation within channelization works in England and Wales'. *Journal of Environmental Management*, 24, 365–382.

Brookes, A. (1987b) 'Restoring the sinuosity of artificially straightened stream channels'. *Environmental Geology and Water Science*, 10, 33–41.

Brookes, A. (1987c) 'The distribution and management of channelized streams in Denmark'. *Regulated Rivers*, 1, 3–16.

Brookes, A. (1988) *Channelized Rivers – Perspectives for Environmental Management.* Wiley: Chichester.

Brookes, A. (1992) 'Recovery and restoration of some engineered British river channels'. In: Boon, P. J., Calow, P. and Petts, G. E. (editors) *River Conservation and Management,* Wiley: Chichester, pp. 407–424.

Brookes, A. (1996) 'River restoration experience in northern Europe'. In: Bookes, A. and Shields, F. D. Jr (editors) *River Channel Restoration: Guiding Principles for Sustainable Projects.* Wiley: Chichester, UK, 233–267.

Brookes, A. and Gregory, K. J. (1988) 'River channelization and public policy'. In: Hooke, J. (editor) *Geomorphology and Environmental Planning.* Wiley: Chichester, 145–167.

Brookes, A., Gregory, K. J. and Dawson, F. H. (1983) 'An assessment of river channelization in England and Wales'. *Science of the Total Environment*, 27, 97–112.

Brookes, A. and Shields, F. D. Jr (1996a) 'Towards an approach to sustainable river restoration'. In: Brookes, A. and Shields, F. D. Jr (editors) *River Channel Restoration, Guiding Principles for Sustainable Projects.* Wiley: Chichester, 385–402.

Brookes, A. and Shields, F. D. Jr (1996b) 'Perspectives on river channel restoration'. In: Brookes, A. and Shields, F. D. Jr (editors) *River Channel Restoration, Guiding Principles for Sustainable Projects.* Wiley: Chichester, 1–19.

Brookes, A., Baker, J. and Redmond, C. (1996) 'Floodplain restoration and riparian zone management'. In: Brookes, A. and Shields, F. D. Jr (editors) *River Channel Restoration, Guiding Principles for Sustainable Projects.* Wiley: Chichester, 201–229.

Brown, A. E. and Howell, D. L. (1992) 'Conservation of rivers in Scotland: legislative and organizational limitations'. In: Boon, P. J., Calow, P. and Petts, G. E. (editors) *River Conservation and Management.* Wiley: Chichester, pp. 407–424.

Budyko, M. I. (1982) *The Earth's Climate: Past and Future.* New York: Academic Press.

Budyko, M. I. and Izrael, Y. A. (1991) *Anthropogenic Climate Change.* Tucson: University of Arizona Press.

Burkham, D. E. (1972) 'Channel changes of the Gila River in Safford Valley, Arizona, 1846–1970'. *United States Geological Survey Professional Paper* 655G, 24 pp.

Campbell, K. L., Kumar, S. and Johnson, H. P. (1972) 'Stream straightening effects on flood runoff characteristics'. *Transactions of the American Society of Agricultural Engineers*, 15, 94–98.

Carbon Dioxide Assessment Committee (1983) *Changing Climate.* Washington, DC: National Academic Press.

Corning, R. V. (1975) 'Channelization: short cut to nowhere'. *Virginia Wildlife*, 6, 8.

Costa, J. E. (1978) 'The dilemma of flood control in the United States'. *Environmental Management*, 2, 313–322.

Dawson, F. H. and Kern-Hansen, U. (1979) 'The effect of natural and artificial shade on the macrophytes of lowland streams and the use of shade as a management technique'. *International Revue Der Gesamten Hydrobiologie*, 64, 437–455.

Downs, P. W., Gregory, K. J. and Brookes, A. (1991) 'How integrated is river basin management?' *Environmental Management,* 15 (3), 299–309.

Edwards, C. J., Griswold, B. L., Tubb, R. A., Weber, E. C. and Woods, L. C. (1984) 'Mitigating effects of artificial riffles and pools on the fauna of a channelised warmwater stream'. *North American Journal of Fisheries Management*, 4, 194–203.

Emanuel, K. A. (1987) 'The dependence of hurricane intensity on climate'. *Nature*, 326, 483–485.

Environment Agency (1996a) *Customer Charter*. Environment Agency for England and Wales, Rivers House, Aztec West, Almondsbury, Bristol BS12 4UD.

Environment Agency (1996b) *The Environment of England and Wales: A Snapshot*. EA: Almondsbury.

Fraedrich, K. (1990) 'European Grosswetter during the warm and cold extremes of the El Niño / Southern Oscillation'. *International Journal of Climatology* 10, 21–31.

Gardiner, J. L. and Cole, L. (1992) 'Catchment planning: The way forward for river protection in the UK'. In: Boon, P. J., Calow, P. and Petts, G. E. (editors) *River Conservation and Management*. Wiley: Chichester, 321–335.

Gardner, R. (1994) 'Environmental degradation in the Himalayas – myth or reality'. Unpublished QMW Geographer, Department of Geography, Queen Mary & Westfield College, University of London, 3.

Glitz, D. (1983) 'Artificial channels – the "ox-bow" lakes of tomorrow: the restoration of the course of the Wandse in Hamburg-Rahlstedt'. *Garten und Landschaft*, 2, 109–111.

Goddard, J. E. (1976) 'The nation's increasing vulnerability to flood catastrophe'. *Journal of Soil and Water Conservation*, 31, 48–52.

Goldstein, N. and Haynes, G. (editors) (1993) *The Flood of '93*. The Associated Press: New York.

Goudie, A. S. (1993) *The Human Impact on the Natural Environment* (fourth edition). Blackwell: Oxford.

Gregory, K. J. and Walling, D. E. (1973) *Drainage Basin Form and Process: a Geomorphological Approach*. Edward Arnold: London.

Gustard, A., Roald, L. A., Demuth, S., Lumadjeng, H. S. and Gross, R. (1989) *Flow Regimes from Experimental and Network Data (FRIEND)*. Institute of Hydrology, 2 volumes.

Hansen, D. R. (1971) *Effects of Stream Channelization on Fishes and Bottom Fauna in the Little Sioux River, Iowa*. Report No. ISDWRRI-38, Iowa State Water Resources Research Institute, Ames, IA.

Haslam, S. M. (1978) *River Plants*. Cambridge University Press: Cambridge.

Haslam, S. M. and Wolseley, P. A. (1981) *River Vegetation: its identification, assessment and management*. Cambridge University Press: Cambridge.

Hedman, E. R. and Osterkamp, W. R. (1982) 'Streamflow characteristics related to channel geometry of streams in Western United States'. *United States Geological Survey, Water Supply Paper*, 2193, Washington DC.

Hemphill, R. W. and Bramley, M. E. (1989) *The Protection of River and Canal Banks. A guide to selection and design*. CIRIA: Butterworths.

Henderson, F. M. and Shields, F. D. (1984) *Environmental Features for Streambank Protection Projects*. Technical Report E-84-11, US Army Engineers Waterways Experiment Station, Vicksburg, MS.

Heuvelmans, M. (1974) *The River Killers*. Stackpole Brooks: Harrisburg, PA.

Hey, R. D. and Thorne, C. R. (1986) 'Stable channels with mobile gravel beds'. *Journal of the Hydraulics Division, American Society of Civil Engineers*, 112, 671–689.

Hilton, R. C. (1979) *Process and Pattern in Physical Geography*. University Tutorial Press: Slough.

Hinge, D. C. and Hollis, G. E. (1980) *Land Drainage, Rivers, Riparian Areas and Conservation*. Discussion Papers in Conservation No. 37, University College London: London.

Holmes, N. T. H. (1995) *Meanderthal ... Bending Rivers Back in Time*. English Nature, pp. 8–9.

Holmes, N. T. H. and Nielsen, M. B. (1998) 'Restoration of the rivers Brede, Cole and Skerne: a joint Danish and British EU LIFE demonstration project, I – Setting up and delivery of the project'. *Aquatic Conservation – Marine and Freshwater Ecosystems*, 8 (1), 185–196.

Horizon (1994) *After the Flood*. Text adapted from the programme transmitted by BBC2 on 18 April 1994.

Houghton, J. T., Kenkins, G. J. and Ephraum, S. J. J. (1990) *Climate Change: the IPCC Scientific Assessment*. Cambridge: Cambridge University Press.

House, M. A. and Sangster, E. K. (1991) 'Public perception of river corridor management'. *Journal of the Institution of Water and Environmental Management*, 5, 312–317.

Ives, J. and Messerli, B. (1989) *The Himalayan Dilemma*. Routledge: London.

Jones, P. D. and Wigley, T. M. L. (1988) *Recent Changes in Precipitation and Precipitation Variability in England and Wales: An update to 1987*. Climate Research Unit, University of East Anglia. Report to WRC.

Jones, P. D., Raper, S. C. B., Bradley, R. S., Diaz, H. F., Kelly, P. M. and Wigley, T. M. L. (1986) 'Northern hemisphere surface air temperature variations, 1851–1984'. *Journal of Climate and Applied Meteorology*, 25, 161–79.

Jutila, E. (1992) 'Restoration of Salmonid rivers in Finland'. In: Boon, P. J., Calow, P. and Petts, G. E. (editors) *River Conservation and Management*. Wiley: Chichester, 353–362.

Keller, E. A. (1976) 'Channelization: environmental, geomorphic and engineering aspects'. In: Coates, D. R. (editor) *Geomorphology and Engineering*. George Allen & Unwin: London, 115–140.

Keller, E. A. (1978) 'Pools, riffles and channelization'. *Environmental Geology*, 2, 119–127.

Keller, E. A. and Brookes, A. (1984) 'Consideration of meandering in channelization projects: selected observations and judgements'. In: *River Meandering, Proceedings of Conference Rivers '83*. American Society of Civil Engineers: Vicksburg, MS, 384–398.

Kern, K. (1992) 'Rehabilitation of streams in south-west Germany'. In: Boon, P. J., Calow, P. and Petts, G. E. (editors) *River Conservation and Management*. Wiley: Chichester, 321–335.

Kern-Hansen, U. (1978) 'The drift of *Gammarus pulex I.* in relation to macrophyte cutting in four small Danish lowland streams'. *Verhandlungen der internationalen Vereinigung für theoretische und angewandte Limnologie*, 20, 1440–1445.

Kimmage, K. and Adams, W. M. (1992) 'Wetland agricultural production and river basin development in the Hadejia-Jama'are Valley, Nigeria'. *The Geographical Journal*, 158 (1), 1–12.

Kirby, C. and White, W. R. (editors) (1994) *Integrated River Basin Development*. Wiley: Chichester.

Knighton, D. (1984) *Fluvial Forms and Processes*. Edward Arnold: London.

Knighton, D. (1998) *Fluvial Forms and Processes: A New Perspective*. Edward Arnold: London.

Kochel, R. C. (1988) 'Geomorphic impact of large floods: Review and new perspectives on magnitude and frequency'. In: Baker, V. R., Kochel, R. C. and Patton, P. C. (editors) *Flood Geomorphology*. Wiley: New York, 169–187.

Kronvang, B., Svendsen, L. M., Brookes, A., Fisher, K., Moller, B., Ottosen, O., Newson, M. and Sear, D. (1998) 'Restoration of the rivers Brede, Cole and Skerne: a joint Danish and British EU LIFE demonstration project, III – Channel morphology, hydrodynamics and transport of sediment and nutrients'. *Aquatic Conservation – Marine and Freshwater Ecosystems*, 8 (1), 209–222.

Lane, S. N. (1995) 'The dynamics of dynamic river channels'. *Geography*, 80 (2), 147–162.

Leopold, L. B. (1977) 'A reverence for rivers'. *Geology*, 5, 429–430.

Lewin, J. (1976) 'Initiation of bedforms and meanders in coarse-grained sediment'. *Bulletin of the Geological Society of America*, 87, 281–285.

Lewis, G. and Williams, G. (1984) *The Rivers and Wildlife Handbook*. RSPB/RSNC: Sandy, Bedfordshire.

Macklin, M. G. and Lewin, J. (1993) 'Holocene river alluviation in Britain'. In: Douglas, I. and Hagedorn, J., *Zeitschrift für Geomorphologie*. Supplement-Band 88, 109–122.

Massachusetts Water Resources Commission (1971) *Neponset River Basin Flood Plain and Wetlands Encroachment Study*. Massachusetts Water Resources Commission: Boston, Massachusetts.

McClellan, T. J. (1974) *Ecological Recovery of Realigned Stream Channels*: Portland, Oregon. Technical Report. Federal Highways Administration, US Department of Transportation, Portland, OR.

Milliman, J. D. and Meade, R. H. (1983) 'World-wide delivery of river sediment to the oceans'. *Journal of Geology*, 91, 1–21.

Mills, G. A. (1981) 'The spawning of roach *Rutilis rutilis*, L. in a chalk stream'. *Fisheries Management*, 12, 49–54.

Morisawa, M. (1985) *Rivers*. Longman: New York.

National Research Council (1992) *Restoration of Aquatic Ecosystems – Science, Technology and Public Policy*. National Academy Press: Washington, DC, USA.

Natural Environment Research Council (1975) *Flood Studies Report*. HMSO: London.

Newson, M. D. (1986) 'River basin engineering – fluvial geomorphology'. *Journal of the Institution of Water Engineers and Scientists*, 40, 307–324.

Newson, M. D. (1992) *Land, Water and Development – River basin systems and their sustainable management*. Routledge: London.

Newson, M. D. (1994) *Hydrology and the River Environment*. Clarendon Press: Oxford.

Newson, M. D. (1997) *Land, Water and Development – Sustainable management of river basin systems* (2nd edn). Routledge: London.

Okidi, C. O. (1990) 'History of the Nile and Lake Victoria Basins through treaties'. In: Howell, P. P. and Allan, J. A. (editors) *The Nile*. SOAS/RGS: London, 193–224.

Palmer, L. (1976) 'River management criteria for Oregon and Washington'. In: Coates, D. R. (editor) *Geomorphology and Engineering*. George Allen & Unwin: London, 329–346.

Palutikov, J. P. (1987) 'Some possible impacts of greenhouse gas-induced climatic change on water resources in England and Wales'. In: *The Influence of Climate Change and Climatic Variability on the Hydrologic Regime and Water Resources*. International Association of Hydrological Sciences, Wallingford: Oxon Publ. 168, 585–596.

Parker, G. and Andres, D. (1976) 'Detrimental effects of river channelization'. *Proceedings of Conference Rivers '76, American Society of Civil Engineers*, 1248–1266.

Parrish, J. D., Maclolek, J. A., Timbol, A. S., Hathaway, C. B. and Norton, S. E. (1978) *Stream Channel Modification in Hawaii. Part D: Summary Report*. Report No. FWS/OBS-78/19, Office of Biological Services, Fish and Wildlife Service, US Department of the Interior, Washington DC.

Petersen, R. C., Petersen, L. B.-M and Lacoursiére, J. (1992) 'A building-block model for stream restoration'. In: Boon, P. J., Calow, P. and Petts, G. E. (editors) *River Conservation and Management*. Wiley: Chichester, 293–309.

Petts, G. E. (1984) *Impounded Rivers: Perspectives for ecological management*. John Wiley and Sons: Chichester, UK.

Purseglove, J. J. (1989) *Taming the Flood – A History and Natural History of Rivers and Wetlands*. Oxford University Press: Oxford.

Reed, D. W. (ed.) (1999) *Flood Estimation Handbook* (in five volumes). Institute of Hydrology: Wallingford, UK.

Revelle, R. R. and Waggoner, P. E. (1983) 'Effect of a carbon dioxide-induced climatic change on water supplies in the western United States'. In: Carbon Dioxide Assessment Committee, *Changing Climate*. Washington, DC: National Academy Press, 419–432.

RSPB, NRA and RSNC (1994) *New Rivers and Wildlife Handbook*. Royal Society for the Protection of Birds: The Lodge, Sandy, Bedfordshire, UK.

Ryckborst, H. (1980) 'Geomorphological changes after river meander surgery'. *Geologie en Mijnbouw*, 59, 121–128.

Schumm, S. A. and Lichty, R. W. (1963) 'Channel widening and flood-plain construction along Cimarron River in south-western Kansas'. *United States Geological Survey Professional Paper*, 352D, 71–88.

Scottish Environment Protection Agency (1996) *Protecting the Quality of Scotland's Environment*. SEPA: Stirling.

Seibert, P. (1968) 'Importance of natural vegetation for the protection of banks of streams, rivers and canals'. *Council of Europe Nature and Environment Series 2*, Freshwater, 35–67.

Shields, F. D. (1983) 'Environmental guidelines for dike fields'. *Proceedings of Conference Rivers '83, American Society of Civil Engineers*, 430–441.

Shields. F. D. and Sanders, T. G. (1986) 'Water quality effects of excavation and diversion'. *Journal of Environmental Engineering, American Society of Civil Engineers*, 112, 211–228.

Soil Conservation Service (1977) 'Compliance with the National Environment Policy Act, 1969; Use of channel modification as a means of water management; and guide for environmental assessment'. *Federal Register*, 42, 40119–40122.

Spillett, P. B. and Armstrong, G. S. (1984) 'Ameliorative methods to reinstate fisheries following land drainage operations'. Paper No. 37 presented at *Symposium of habitat modification and freshwater fisheries*. European Inland Fisheries Advisory Commission, Thirteenth Session. Arhus, Denmark.

Stanners, D. and Bourdeau, P. (editors) (1995) *Europe's Environment: The Döbris Assessment*, prepared by the European Agency Task Force (European Commission: DXXI and Phare), European Environment Agency, Copenhagen, Denmark.

Stern, P. C., Young, O. R. and Druckman, D. (editors) (1992) *Global Environmental Change – Understanding the Human Dimensions*. Washington, DC: National Academy Press.

Swales, S. (1980) 'Investigations of the effects of river channel works on the ecology of fish populations'. Unpublished PhD thesis, University of Liverpool, UK.

Swales, S. (1982a) 'A "before and after" study of the effects of land drainage works on fish stocks in the upper reaches of a lowland river'. *Fish Management*, 13, 105–113.

Swales, S. (1982b) 'Environmental effects of river channel works used in land drainage improvements'. *Journal of Environmental Management*, 14, 103–126.

Tuckfield, C. G. (1980) 'Stream channel stability and forest drainage in the New Forest, Hampshire'. *Earth Surface Processes*, 5, 317–379.

Vanoni, V. A. (editor) (1975) *Sedimentation Engineering*. Manuals and reports on engineering practice No. 54, American Society of Civil Engineers, New York.

Vivash, R., Ottosen, O., Jones, M. and Sorensen, H. V. (1998) 'Restoration of the rivers Brede, Cole and Skerne: a joint Danish and British EU LIFE demonstration project, II – The river restoration works and other related practical aspects'. *Aquatic Conservation – Marine and Freshwater Ecosystems* 8 (1), 197–208.

Walsh, R. P., Hudson, R. N. and Howells, K. A. (1982) 'Changes in the magnitude-frequency of flooding and heavy rainfall in the Swansea Valley sinece 1875'. *Cambria* 9 (2), 36–60.

Ward, R. C. (1978) *Floods: A Geographical Perspective*. Macmillan Press Ltd: London.

Wharton, G. (1995) 'The channel-geometry method: guidelines and applications'. *Earth Surface Processes and Landforms*, 20, 649–660.

White, R. J. (1968) 'So baut man Forellenunterständ'. *Ein Schwerpunkt der Bachpflege* (Creating shelters for trout: a stream management). Verlag Paul Parey: Hamburg and Berlin.

Wigley, T. M. L., Jones, P. D. and Kelly, P. M. (1980) 'Scenario for a warm, high-CO_2 world'. *Nature*, 283, 17–21.

Winkley, B. R. (1982) 'Response of the lower Mississippi to river training and realignment'. In: Hey, R. D., Bathurst, J. C. and Thorne, C. R. (editors) *Gravel-bed Rivers*. John Wiley and Sons: Chichester, UK, 652–681.

Wolman, M. G. and Gerson, R. (1978) 'Relative scales of time and effectiveness of climate in watershed geomorphology'. *Earth Surface Processes*, 3, 189–208.

Wyzga, B. (1996) 'Changes in the magnitude and transformation of flood waves subsequent to the channelization of the Raba River, Polish Carpathians'. *Earth Surface Processes and Landforms*, 15, 45–53.

Yearke, L. W. (1971) 'River erosion due to channel relocation'. *Civil Engineering*, 41, 39–40.

Index